FRED'S RULES
(AND A FEW WISHES)

DON FEDERIC

COUNTRY BOOKS/ASHRIDGE PRESS

Published by Country Books/Ashridge Press
Country Books, Courtyard Cottage, Little Longstone,
Bakewell, Derbyshire DE45 1NN

Tel/Fax: 01629 640670
e-mail: dickrichardson@country-books.co.uk

ISBN 978 1 901214 87 1

By the same author:
AN ADULT STOCKING FILLER –
A VERY VARIABLE DOZEN

Printed and bound by: HSW Print.

CONTENTS

FOREWORD

Hopefully this introduction will follow, at least in principle, the advice given to after dinner speakers to "stand up, speak up and shut up."

Again, hopefully humorously, the following few lines will indicate a latent personality trait essentially needed to write a book such as this.

Early in the 1960s, living on an irrigation research farm in the Sabi Valley area of Southern Rhodesia my wife, two friends and two visitors were playing a card or board game after dinner, I cannot remember which.

The research farm was well and truly "in the sticks" or "in the bush" and television had not arrived, consequently in whiling away leisure time after dark recourse was often made to cards or dice controlled board games.

One of the visitors was new to the game we were playing and in the middle of it I offered her a few tips. She, in fact, was a very switched on modern miss and she said very sweetly "Would you like to play my game as well?" Ho! Ho! point well made.

Some forty plus years later a close friend or relative, oh memory wherefore art thou?, coined the phrase "Fred's rules", this followed a discourse from me on changes I would like to see.

In recent months I decided to put pen to paper on the subject of proposing changes to rules and laws as well as listing a few wishes and then to stand back, as it were, and wonder if they were not too cranky to publish; time will tell on both of those points.

At this stage let me state very firmly that 1 am not at all chauvinistic with regard to gender. In fact I am a great admirer of women on many counts and I am appalled at how they are treated in many areas of the world. I have been very happily married for fifty six years and my wife and I have been blessed with three daughters and a son, in that order. I make this point ladies in explanation for mainly using the male gender in the following text.

This is because it does not tax my grasp of English grammar by using they or their etc etc.

Although many of the games I have covered probably started out as the exclusive pursuits of men they are now anything but that and very good luck to the ladies who now play them.

FOOTBALL

There are several reasons for the proposals I will put forward regarding changing existing or introducing new rules for the game.

By far the major reason is to try and make it easier to score goals and hence reduce the number of games that result in draws in league-type games or penalty shoot-outs in cup competitions.

Other reasons are to reduce the amount of time wasting and negative type play, which may be taking place under the guise of tactics, and hence make it more interesting and enjoyable for nearly all concerned.

I thought about the majority of these proposed changes some seventeen years ago, nothing that has happened since has changed my basic thinking.

I played at school and also for a few months, at the age of twenty-six, in Southern Rhodesia. I played at right half or right wing; looking back my skills were mediocre in the extreme but I enjoyed playing which surely is a good enough reason for partaking.

Circa 1949 or 1950 I saw Tottenham Hotspur, at home, play Newcastle. I think it was in one of the rounds of the FA cup.

The whole ground was very wet and the general area in front of at least one of the goals was a quagmire. Early in the match the Spurs goalkeeper ran out to meet the ball and fell flat on his back! Strong kicks were needed to get the ball airborne and once it hit the mud it barely moved – were those the days?

From the comparative remoteness of Central Africa I generally supported any of the London clubs in the leagues or cup, that is to say I was interested in football but not fanatically so.

In 1990 I watched many of the world cup games on television and followed the results with great interest, more especially of the group in which England was playing.

The exact results and scores of the games in that group are not to hand as I write this (January 2007) but at the time I noted that very few goals were scored and many of the games resulted in draws.

This turn of events must have interested or irked me to the extent that I wrote to FIFA and suggested many changes in the rules/laws governing football aimed at making it easier to score goals and thereby, hopefully, decreasing the number of matches ending in draws.

Subsequently I received a nice letter from the General Secretary of FIFA, Mr J S Blatter – the letter was dated October 1990. This letter of thanks for the interest I had shown was accompanied by a FIFA souvenir and a separate sheet of A4 paper listing proposals submitted to FIFA following "Italia 90". The souvenir, a small silver lapel badge, I gave to a friend who happened to be an FA qualified referee and the statistics are given below:

FIFA
FEDERATION INTERNATIONALE DE FOOTBALL ASSOCIATION
LETTERS SENT TO FIFA REGARDING "ITALIA '90"

Recapitulation statistics		
Total letters received	396	
Proposals	Total	
Changing World Cup System	146	
Elimination of decision by penalty kicks	144	*
Changing or eliminating the offside rule	40	*
Remarks regarding referees	35	*
Changing points system	43	
Increasing the size of the goal	71	*
Timekeeping	21	
Fewer players	17	
Changing the system of prolongation	57	*
Kick-in instead of throw-in	6	*
No return pass to the goalkeeper allowed	13	*
No walls in free-kick situations	3	*
More substitute players	5	

Various proposals regarding the Laws of the game   70   *
Total proposals   671
Zurich, 24.10.1990
The * indicates that I had submitted a proposal in that context.

Unfortunately I do not have a complete copy of my original letter to FIFA in 1990 immediately available but the gist of it is as follows:-

In my opinion far too many first class matches end in draws, very often without a single goal being scored.

Teams are locked in combat for the full ninety minutes and, in cup matches, this can be followed by another thirty minutes of extra time again with no score.

Goals, in many cases, are so hard to come by that when a team scores one they have a tendency to go into a defensive mode. The modern game has been analysed in the greatest depth and obviously defensive strategies have been at least planned.

The following suggestions are aimed at making it easier to score goals and/or improve the game for both spectators and, hopefully, players.

Football today is big business, very, very big business. Many players are paid salaries that cause one's mind to boggle but, as the saying goes, "that is how the cookie has crumbled." Nevertheless it is essential, in my opinion, that for the spectators and fans sake every effort must be made to provide them with top rate entertainment in the form of more goals, less draws and much less time wasting.

The final wording of the following proposals, if used, needs to be simple, clear and unambiguous.

PROPOSAL ONE

This proposal is rather <u>drastic</u> but, I feel, <u>absolutely essential</u>.

A player must not pass the ball backwards in or into his own half of the field. The wording could be something to the effect that while in his own half of the field any pass or attempted pass made must have a clearly visible forward component, the advantage rule should be applied if needed.

This suggestion is made to stop the inherent time wasting employed by practically all teams, even more so if they are leading, when the ball is passed backward and forward ad lib in or into their own half of the field. Granted there can be a tactical reason for this type of play insofar as it may be planned to draw the other team's players forward but, in my opinion, it is frustrating in the extreme and could well be construed as time wasting or extremely negative play.

There will, I am sure, be positive results from such a proposal, if a player is in possession of the ball in his own half of the field he will not be able to assume that he will not be tackled, he will have to pass the ball forward or move forward with it and hope to beat any attacking player approaching him. In many cases there may be two or more players converging on him because his own players who are behind him can, at that stage, be disregarded by the attacking players.

Other positives are that the defending player will have to develop his ball retaining skills and increase the accuracy of his passing. The attacking player, usually a forward, will have to develop his tackling skills.

In avoiding a player tackling him the defender may take the ball back while trying to retain possession or control of it but another defender cannot intercept a ball that does not have a clearly visible forward component to its travel. Summing up if a defending player makes contact with a ball in his own half of the field he must try to retain control of it or pass it in a forward direction.

The grass on many football pitches is cut in parallel strips across the field, at right angles to the touch lines. Up to a point the narrower these strips are the more use they will be to the match officials. Such visible strips must also be useful in offside decisions.

PROPOSAL TWO

I think that something better than "Penalty Shoot Outs" must be devised. My reasoning for this is that I think that individual players should not be subjected to the intense mental strain of having to kick penalty type goals in such a cold-blooded way. Football is a hot-blooded game and does not deserve such endings. In one world cup final one of the world's top forwards put his kick straight over the crossbar as an example of the intense pressure the players are subject to.

Other ways of deciding the winning team when the scores are level must be considered, such as:

Two A   Large clocks situated roughly in line with the halfway line should display the amount of time the ball is in the respective halves of the pitch, the winning team, in a draw situation, will be the one which has kept the ball longest in their opponent's half of the field. This could be depicted by hands on the clock or by the minutes and seconds being displayed next to the names of the teams. A refinement of this method could be the amount of time the ball is in the respective "PENALTY ZONES", this expression will be explained later.

Two B   The team taking the most corners wins.

Two C   The team whose goalkeeper handles the ball the least number of times wins.

Two D   The team taking the least number of free kicks wins.

Two E   If a penalty shoot-out is deemed necessary it should be taken before the match starts.

Two F   As a variation of Two A the large clocks could display the amount of time each team is in possession of the ball; the team in possession the longest wins. Not easy to calculate but in this electronic age not impossible.

Two G   In cup matches such as World, European, Asian, South African, FA and other continental or national knock-out competitions consideration should be given to the team's performance in reaching a particular stage of the competition, for example, during the group stages or early rounds. This can be refined once a team reaches the knock out matches or the eighth or quarter final stage. Performance can be based on goals for and against, number of corners awarded or number of free kicks.Consideration could be given to a system used in chess whereby the points awarded can be reassessed in regard to the calibre of the player played against, the Buchholtz system.

        The crux of the matter is that in each match of a cup contest the teams should know that in the event of a draw in goals after full time or after full time plus extra time which of them will win. The desirability of leaving the final grading until the knock out stage or quarter finals is based on the fact that in the earlier rounds there may well be one or two very weak teams against which a good team may do exceptionally well and hence enhance their goal average or total corner kicks

In all of the methods suggested the potential winner in a drawing situation is known by the spectators and players and this will result in a greater effort to achieve victory by scoring a goal. This statement can be justified by considering the changed urgency to score when one team scores and takes the lead, in many such situations this injection of urgency to score is immediately obvious.

Two or more of the suggested methods, with the exception of Two E can be used in a prearranged system of priority, for example:

RESULT IN EVENT OF DRAW DECIDED BY:
Two B   Most corner kicks
IF EQUAL
Two C   Number of times handled by goalkeeper
IF ALSO EQUAL
Two A   Amount of time in opponents half of pitch

PROPOSAL THREE
The offside law should be changed. It was, I think, originally introduced to stop "GOALHANGERS", these were attacking players who waited close to the goal for the ball to arrive, often from a long range kick.

I propose that the actual penalty area should be left as it is but the transverse line should be extended each way to meet the touch lines. The area between that whole line and goal line could be known as the penalty zone

The offside law should be changed so that an attacking player should not be deemed offside if the ball is kicked to him from within the penalty zone. The normal offside rule applies to a ball kicked from outside the penalty zone.

My reasoning for this is one can see the situation where a player is deemed offside to a ball kicked only a few yards from the goal line. I am sure the law was not intended for such close range situations.

The expression "Offside Trap" sums up what is often a rather sneaky situation in my opinion.

Football is a great game, players can display several different types of skill to a greater or lesser degree and how entertaining it can be watching those skills being shown and utilised at all levels of play from junior leagues right up to the world cup. In this regard how annoying it can be to see a brilliantly exciting and fluid passing and advancing attack cut short by the whistle blowing for an offside infringement to a pass sent from a player who is only a few yards from the goal line.

PROPOSAL FOUR

In as many matches as possible there should be six match officials on the pitch, two referees, essentially one 'patrols' one half of the pitch and, basically but not exclusively, adjudicates on the play in that half of the pitch. The other four officials effectively are responsible for half of one touch line each.

Very strong consideration should be given to three off the pitch officials to whom reference may be made for help in situations of doubt that can possibly be resolved by studying television replays. This facility can also be utilised for off the ball incidents.

The cost involved in establishing this proposal in top flight matches would only be a very small percentage of the total revenue generated.

PROPOSAL FIVE

Following the 1990 World Cup matches 71 people suggested that the size of the goal should be increased, one of these people was me.

I understand that this was done; it would be interesting to know if any statistics can be referred to as to any effect this had. In any event the size of the goal could be increased again slightly, say one metre wider, more goals and fewer draws are both desirable. We do not want the situation where rugby type scores are possible but in general more goals are needed.

PROPOSAL SIX

When the ball goes out of play over a touch line a kick-in may be taken instead of a throw-in. The ball must be placed on the touch line to indicate that it is going to be kicked back into play; time must be allowed for the players to reposition themselves before the ball is kicked back into play from its position on the touch line.

The reason for this proposal is to encourage the players to keep the ball in play. The offside rule should be waived for the actual kick-in. In desperate defending situations the player will think twice about deliberately tapping the ball over the touch line.

PROPOSAL SEVEN

A free-kick awarded to a team in their own half of the field must be taken in the normal way governed by the existing rules. A free kick awarded to a team in their opponents half may be taken in the normal way or it may be taken in a proposed new way that, amongst other things, will dispense with the defensive wall. Disregarding the player taking the kick and the defending goalkeeper all other players must be at least ten yards from the ball. In addition no player except the goalkeeper must be in the triangle formed by the goal line and the lines that could be drawn from each corner flag to the ball. This is shown in the diagram. It is not so complicated as it sounds as it will be comparatively easy to monitor; a match official will go to each corner flag and hold up an arm horizontally pointing to the ball. Under the present rules it takes time to get the 'wall' the required distance from the ball. Again the offside rule does not apply to the actual free kick.

PROPOSAL EIGHT

To review corner kick rules. The situation can arise whereby a defender in a desperate situation kicks the ball over the goal line fairly close to the goal. To penalise the defending team the ball is taken out to the corner flag; this, in my opinion, is penalising the attacking team. To counter this I suggest that a 'corner kick' may be taken from where the ball went over the line or from such point anywhere further away from the goal along the goal line or on the touch line on that side of the field as chosen by the attacking team. Again all players other than the goalkeeper or the man taking the kick must be at least ten yards from the ball. If the ball goes out of play over the bar due to a defending player then the corner kick may be taken from the point where the penalty area side line meets the goal line or such point further out along the line as selected by the attacking team.

PROPOSAL NINE

If a defending player, other than the goalkeeper, stops the ball with his hand from crossing the goal line into the goal the referee should consider awarding a goal instead of a penalty. For the referee to award a goal he must be convinced beyond all doubt that a goal would have been scored but for the defender handling the ball whether such handling was deliberate or accidental. If the referee considers that the handling was accidental the player should not be shown a red or a yellow card.

The referee can/must seek the views of the other match officials, on or off the field, before making any decision final, be it for awarding a goal or not penalising the player who accidentally handled the ball.

PROPOSAL TEN

The law as regards time wasting is to be applied in obvious cases when the ball is in play. A particular example of this can be seen when an attacking team, who are leading on goals scored, are awarded a corner. The man taking it taps it to a member of his team who promptly taps it back to him, these two players then contrive to keep possession of the ball in that corner of the pitch. This often takes place in the last few minutes of play.

Another example of blatant time wasting, in my opinion, is when the ball is repeatedly passed to and fro in a team's own half of the pitch. I have suggested a counter to this in Proposal One but if this is not adopted then such tactics should be regarded as time wasting, which they are.

GENERAL OBSERVATIONS

I think that shirt pulling, or pushing, need to be watched for and punished immediately and also the jostling in free kick or corner kick situations needs to be frowned on, no bodily contact should be allowed although it will not be easy in all cases to see who the offender is.

I think that the game needs a shake up as it is becoming too predictable and stereotyped.

Football is a great game, no doubt the same thing can be said, with justification, about other games and sports. The words game and sport are, in many cases, interchangeable. Athletics, for example, are sports yet we have the Olympic Games but recourse to a dictionary yields: GAME: an activity engaged in for amusement. SPORT: an activity involving physical exertion and skill in which an individual or team competes against another or others for entertainment.

Two of the words that form one link between GAME and SPORT are amusement and entertainment. Football can rightly be described as a game or as a sport. These two words should be kept in very sharp focus; football is a GAME yet it is all too easy to lose sight of the word GAME in today's hyped up world.

I have seen photographs of young fans, and sometimes not-so-young fans, in tears when THEIR team has not won a critical cup or league match. This fact, the emotion, made me wonder with some concern as to why the young fan was so moved by the result of a GAME which should have been for amusement. Players can sometimes be seen in tears following a loss. My wonder at this emotion led me to think "Has that young fan nothing better to expend such emotion on?" IT IS A GAME

Against the assertion that football is a GAME a person has to wonder about the violence that often accompanies football games and fans. A photograph of a policeman with a dart sticking in his head, numerous absolutely tragic injuries and deaths. The most recent death, as these words are penned, being that of a policeman in Italy.

Hot off the press, as the saying goes, is a brief report on a fight between the reserve team players of a famous club and a visiting international side; what harm has that done to football, to sport and to international relations? For the true enjoyment of the GAME of football it is absolutely essential that an answer is found to such on and off the pitch violence.

A drawing and explanation of the proposed changes follows:

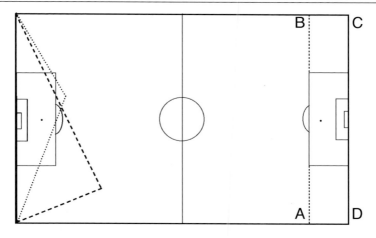

Proposed changes to laws governing offside, free kicks and corner kicks.

OFFSIDE

The line parallel to the goal line marking the edge of the penalty area shall be extended as a solid white line to meet the touch lines at A and B. The lines parallel to the touch line marking the edges of the penalty area shall remain as they are.

The area enclosed by ABCD shall be known as the penalty zone or (???). A player attacking the goal in the penalty zone cannot be offside to a ball that is kicked from inside that penalty zone

CORNER KICKS

A "Corner" kick may be taken from on the goal line where the ball went out of play or at some point, further away from goal, along the goal line or the touch line on that side of the field as chosen by the attacking team.

FREE KICKS

A free kick awarded to a team in their own half of the field must be taken in the normal way. A free kick awarded to a team in their opponents half of the field may be taken in the normal way or in the following way as chosen by the attacking team.

Two examples are given on the drawing. Essentially imaginary lines run from the ball to each corner flag. Only the goalkeeper is allowed in the triangle formed by the goal line and the two imaginary lines. All other defending players must be at least ten yards from the ball and must not move into the triangle until the ball has been kicked. Similarly attacking players are not allowed into the triangle until the ball has been kicked.

Goal scoring chances should be enhanced by this proposed change particularly if the no offside rule to a ball kicked from within the penalty zone is also adopted. It will be a challenge to exploit the opportunities to best advantage.

TENNIS

This chapter was prompted by the fixed conviction that the server in today's circumstances has <u>much too great</u> an advantage and that the game, for most players and most spectators, will benefit enormously by eliminating the advantage that the server has.

Essentially the server can control three aspects of the dynamics of the ball after it leaves his racquet. Its direction, its speed and its rotation, ie its spin.

The receiver has to position himself where he thinks best to counter these three basic aspects of the ball's dynamics as it comes towards him.

All of these aspects can cause problems and he positions himself using his knowledge of his opponent's ability and his own skill in returning the ball effectively.

In recent years it has become apparent that some of the best players in the world are being beaten by services which they fail to reach. All three aspects of the ball's dynamics contribute towards this but the main obstacle faced by the receiver is to position himself to cover all possible directions of the ball, ie. on his backhand or on his forehand.

Going off at, hopefully, an interesting aside here by stating that in studying dynamics SPEED and VELOCITY are not the same thing; speed only implies speed but velocity implies speed and direction and so one can say that the velocity of the ball has to be judged and countered by the receiver.

Hopefully many people will agree with my contention that something has to be done about the excessive advantage that the server has in today's game.

The way to erode this advantage is to reduce the VELOCITY of the ball. This can be done by reducing its speed or by restricting its direction.

This can be accomplished by altering the specification of ball and/or racquet, by altering the dimensions of the court and/or net, by restricting the number of services and/or by where the server must stand to serve. There may well be other ways that I have not thought of.

In solving the problem one must not curtail the ability of a player to hit the ball as hard as he likes and the service should not be watered down so much that the receiver has a clear cut advantage.

My favoured solution is to limit the angle that the receiver has to cover by altering the shape of the service box. Incidentally this suggestion should help older or slightly handicapped players to enjoy the game more.

Depending on which method is chosen to limit the angle it may also limit the speed, albeit slightly; my chosen way will have no noticeable limiting effect on the speed at which the ball is hit.

In my era, as a teenager, tennis was considered, if one thought about it at all, to be rather a cissy sort of game. This of course is a top scoring "How can one be so wrong?"

At the age of twenty in 1946 I first held a racquet in my hand and hit a tennis ball on a tennis court. That was during my army service in India.

The next time was when I was working for the Forestry Commission in the Eastern district of Southern Rhodesia. Several of us, weather permitting, used to play in the evening after work, that was circa 1957/58. There were a couple of good players there, one of them particularly made the game look so easy, he was also a scratch golfer!, a natural ball player, lucky man. On that theme my wife and I have three sons-in-law, two of them are also natural ball players, the third one we have not seen in action yet.

I make this point because there are many people with a natural talent for "stick and ball" games but how many of them have been denied the opportunity to progress because no facilities or coaches were/are available to encourage them?

For about forty plus years my wife and I played social tennis in various country clubs in Southern Rhodesia and Zimbabwe. Neither of us had received any coaching and, in my case, it must have shown because I eventually realised that I did not have the effortless basic ground strokes that are so necessary as a platform on which to build. It is a great game from several points of view, for example, socially and keeping fit.

As stated previously, in recent years I think an imbalance has developed in the advantage gained by the player serving. Several factors contribute towards this, one of them being the general increase in the height of players and another the improved efficiency of racquets.

The end result has been, in my opinion, that too many games are won mainly due to a receiving player not even getting his racquet to the ball. I think I am right in stating that the authorities at Wimbledon introduced "slower" balls.

Surely the service is, or should be, just a means of getting the ball into play and giving both players an equal chance of winning the point. How good it is to see the ball in play with both players showing their all round skills and stamina to best advantage and, at the top level, what skills these are! There are barely enough superlatives to describe them. The recent final in the Australian Open between Roger Federer and Fernando Gonzales produced some truly amazing winning points to end long rallies. THIS IS WHAT THE GAME SHOULD BE ABOUT. It should not be about walking backwards and forwards along the baseline smashing in ace services.

One just has to consider how many games are won by the player serving and how much importance is given to "breaking" a service; very often it is vital in deciding who wins the game, the set or the match. The proposals I have suggested will not result in slower services, the server will still be able to display his mastery of that phase of the game but they will give the receiver more chance to at least get a racquet to the ball and control the return shot.

If the advantage gained by serving is negated this will also level the playing field in tie break situations. Such levelling may result in longer games, possibly leading to longer sets. In Grand Slam type of events this could be offset by reducing the number of sets from five to three, possibly in all matches except the final.

So how to so curtail the advantage possessed by the server without passing the advantage to the receiver? I, naturally, advocate my

Proposal One as follows:

PROPOSAL ONE

The service box/area should be made narrower by moving the outside line in to achieve this. Note that I am not suggesting that the whole court should be made narrower, just the service box. The result of this will be that the receiver does not have such a wide area/arc to cover, ie the receiver should at least be able to make contact with the ball without setting himself up for the coup-de-grace of a serve and volley exponent.

The server will still be able to hit the ball practically as hard as he likes but the receiver stands more chance of returning the serve.

The drawing shows how a court would be marked for such a proposal. As the court dimensions are specified in Imperial units of measure I suggest that the line should be moved in four or five feet, in the drawing it is moved in four feet in one of the "boxes" and five feet in another box. Subsequent experience should show how effective these suggested changes are at eroding the advantage at present held by the server.

The line judge at the receiving end will be able to position himself to look down the outside line of the box for the serve and then move sideways to align with the outside line, if this movement proved to distract the player or players at the "serving" end of the court more judges can be used, there should not be a problem.

In the drawing I have shown two other ways to mark the service box. These will pose problems for the line judges as their view of the action may not be ideal.

Another method suggested has been to limit the server to one attempt, a variation of this would be to allow the server to have one (or two?) second attempts per game. Interestingly why should the server be allowed two attempts at serving?, this is rather ramming home the advantage. If this passes the advantage to the receiver why not specify where the receiver has to stand to receive the service, ho! ho!, pardon the pun, a whole new ball game.

Yet another way would be to put an extra service line, say four or five feet back from the base line while leaving the other court dimensions as they are; this would slightly limit the horizontal and vertical angles of the serve and give the receiver more time to move to cover the angle. For a 100 MPH service five feet would give the receiver an extra 0,0341 seconds to cover the angle and also it would very slightly reduce the pace at which the ball arrives. It would also entail that a serve and volley exponent would have slightly less time to reach the net.

There are other ways to limit the advantage gained by serving without passing the advantage to the receiver, one would be to specify that the serve must be from a particular area; this I have explained in the drawing. I had not thought about it before I started to write these proposals but I think it has merit.

Another two ways would be to specify that the server must serve with both feet on the ground, or to increase the height of the net, but, the first of these would feel unnatural and would not be easy to judge, the second would slow the whole game down, not desirable.

Yet another way which has just surfaced in my mind is also shown, this will be easier to comprehend by looking at the drawing, as I type this I get the distinct feeling that it is the answer, apart from fixing the dimensions. The service box will have the same length as present but there will not be a centre line. It will be centrally situated and fourteen feet wide. There will be short lines on the base lines in line with the lines of the service box. The player serving may serve from anywhere on the base line between the two short lines. This will ensure that the receiver will not have to cover an impossible angle and he will not be too far out to cover a return from a serve and volley specialist. The dimension to fix to ensure a fair start to the game will be the width of the service box. Note that there will be no question of a fixed routine of the service alternating from the different sides of the court as at present. The serve may be from anywhere between the marks on the base line.

I have not thought this through for doubles yet but I will work on it.

Essentially the same argument regarding the advantage possessed by the server applies to doubles. Ho! Ho! I have thought it through, let them get on with it, as in singles the server will not find it easy to serve aces therefore the ball will be in play more often and this should please everyone except the server. Just had another thought, the last (I promise!) on this matter. In modem parlance "Lateral thinking". Why not leave the court dimensions for doubles exactly as they are for singles?, that is to say there will be no tramlines. The top players will still find ways of winning points even though the games should last longer. A good spin off will occur in social doubles in so far as older players will be able to reach the ball more often.

It is interesting to wonder how the court dimensions regarding singles and doubles were decided on in the first place. One thing is for sure and that is the administrators then would have had no idea of the world wide interest in the game brought about by television coverage

Drawings and explanations of the proposals suggested can be seen on pages 24 and 25.

PROPOSAL TWO

At the moment each of the countries putting on a Grand Slam open event incorporate doubles matches and crowns, in some cases, particularly on account of the weather, this can result in time pressure to fit them all in. Also, of course, many of the world's top singles players do not enter any of the doubles competitions.

I propose that every year World Doubles Championships should be held. The dates for such an event should be chosen so as not to cause the Grand Slam venues any problems. Every year one of these venues should be selected to host the championships. This, I think, would give doubles players the better exposure that they richly deserve.

While on the subject of Grand Slams surely the time must be approaching when other countries Opens will deserve to be one of the Grand Slams.

As a final observation let me observe that if the rules are changed to limit the perceived advantage gained by serving then whoever wins the toss/spin of racquet may elect to receive and not as is normally done to serve, that is to say if the perceived advantage is passed to the receiver then the player winning the toss will elect to receive and not to serve first. This is an interesting "Proof of the Pudding" test.

And, to end, please LIMIT THE ADVANTAGE OF SERVING AND GET MORE ACTUAL TENNIS.

The dimensions of a tennis court are specified in Imperial feet and for a "Singles" court the length is 78 feet and the width is 27 feet. The line marking the in court transverse edge of the "Service Box" is 21 feet from the net.

The drawing seems to show an elongated court but this is due to two factors, one being that it is a single's court and secondly the telephoto lenses of television cameras tend to foreshorten distances.

On this drawing the services are assumed to be taken from the usual places and four different proposals are shown. It is heavily stressed that each box or service position would be reproduced symmetrically so that the whole court is balanced. The different proposals have been shown on the same court, hopefully the method should not be confusing but they can be compared, At this point it is worth noting that very tall players stand much more chance of serving at greater angles, particularly when serving into the outside corners of the service boxes. It would be very interesting and enlightening to know how high the ball is, on average, when hit by various players when serving.

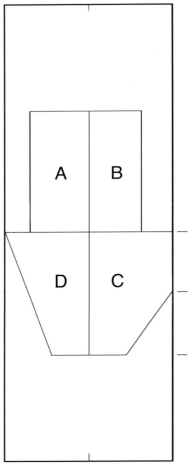

The outside line of service box A has been moved in 4 feet.

The outside line of service box B has been moved in 5 feet.

In service box C the diagonal across the corner of the box ends at the middle point of the lines it touches.

In service box D the diagonal runs from the "end" of the net along a line from that point projected to the centre of the baseline, in all cases the service box has not been shortened. The server can hit the ball as hard as he likes but the angle that the receiver has to cover has been reduced.

A ruler or similar straightedge can be used to give one an idea of the angle that has to be covered when the service is delivered from any legal point on the baseline into the extreme corners of the service boxes as shown on the drawing. These angles can be compared to those possible through me corners of normal service boxes.

In the half of the court with the service box K there is no centre line. The service box K is 15 feet wide, this is 1·5 feet wider than the normal service box but the box is centrally situated. The services into this box (K) must be from the baseline between the lines marked "k"; these lines are also 15 feet apart and centrally situated. This is a departure from the established practice of alternating the services between the forehand and backhand sides of the court. To further limit the angle available the lines "k" could each be moved in two feet towards the centre line of the court as shown at "k1" while leaving the service box width at 15 feet as suggested, the reasoning behind this is to restrict the angle that can be gained due to the server hitting the ball while leaning outwards, that is to say the server's feet may be in a legal position but his racquet when it makes contact with the ball could be outside the short line marking the end of the service line. This particularly applies to a right handed player serving at the right end of the serving line or a left-handed one serving from the left end of the line.

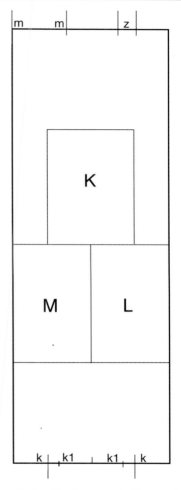

In the other half of the court the service boxes are exactly the same size as normal. Two different suggestions are put forward as to where the service must be delivered from. Each of these suggestions is a radical departure from normal insofar as the service must be delivered into the service box on the same side of the court as the server, this is explained as follows. The service into box M is from the baseline between the lines marked "m", these lines are 9 feet apart.

The service into box L is from the box on the baseline marked "1". As shown in the drawing box "1" is 3 feet wide and is situated 4·5 feet from the centre line and 6 feet from the outside line of the court, these dimensions could be altered to make this box slightly larger or to reposition it a little. In the proposals as depicted in the drawings it should be borne in mind that the primary objective is to reduce the angle that the receiver has to cover and thereby limit the distance he has to move outside the projected sidelines of the court just to get his racquet to the ball.

CRICKET

I played the game at school when aged about twelve or thirteen and also at different stages and ages as an adult both in the UK and in Southern Rhodesia. With hindsight I had no star quality potential but at different times I did bowl and open the batting. This I hasten to add should be taken in the context of the level of play pertaining in a friendly Saturday afternoon league.

At times, when a team was short of a player or two I was exposed to a higher level of play in a country districts league match. I was keen enough to practice as often as I could; at the end of this article on cricket I will put an idea forward with regard to training.

In different locations I have followed test match commentaries on the radio and/or television. Back in 1953/56 in Southern Rhodesia a radio known as a "Saucepan" radio was available, so called because it had a metal case and it looked like a medium-size saucepan. It stood on a large dry battery, not rechargeable, the cost of the battery £1.50 in those days, was fairly high. It had very good short wave reception and right out in the bush we could follow Australia and England battling out an Ash's series; do I correctly recall Ray Lindwall scoring a century as a tail ender?

The following proposals are made with a view to levelling the playing field and making the game more enjoyable for spectators and possibly for the players as well.

PROPOSAL ONE

That all of the test playing nations' captains have one "ceremonial toss" and that gives the winning captain of that nation's team the choice of batting or fielding in the next test match played between those two nations. From that game onwards the choice will alternate. This will ensure that in a test series the chance of one captain being lucky and winning the toss four or even five times is ruled out. In the next series the choice is made by the captain that did not have the choice in the game at the end of the last series.

Games totally written off due to weather will not count. This proposal is made because "winning the toss" can often be very advantageous.

The "Ceremonial Toss" could be amongst all of the current captains in one location at the same time or in a link-up between the various capitals, in either case it could be televised and/or broadcast. Perhaps a sponsor could be found? The same procedure could be followed for One Day Internationals.

PROPOSAL TWO

I should think that in some form or other this proposal has been thought about previously as it is a rather obvious variation of the basic form in which the game is played. In general the objective is to arrange for each team to occupy the crease for the same amount of time unless:

(A)   One of the teams declares, in which case they <u>will not bat again</u> and their opponents can occupy the crease until the end of the normal playing time or until, in the normal playing time, a result is obtained, ie they pass their opponents total or they are all out before reaching that total. Note that if play takes place until the end of the actual playing time it will be possible for the result to be a tie if the scores are level.

(B)   The second innings of a team ends, in which case the other team can occupy the crease until the end of normal playing time or until a result is obtained.

(C)   It should be possible to devise a method similar to the Duckworth Lewis formula to decide which team has won in the event of the weather not permitting play to continue to the normal finishing time. This is to suggest that a draw is not a possible result, matches will either be won or tied. Thought should be given to any other method of deciding which team wins in the situation described above. For example dividing the total number of runs scored by the number of legal balls bowled, that is to say runs per ball, no balls and wides would not count as balls bowled but runs scored off them would be included in the total runs scored. The team with the highest average runs per ball would win the match. Another way would be to divide the number of runs scored by the number of minutes the side was batting, runs per minute. The method chosen should be the one least capable of being "juggled" in a way contrary to the spirit of the game.

The proposal firstly envisages that each day is split up into three periods of two hours each. The starting time will be chosen so as to ensure that in normal weather conditions six hours actual play can be easily achieved. In different locations the starting times could vary, the table below assumes three different locations A, B and C.

LOCATIONS

PERIODS	A	B	C
FIRST	09.30 to 11.30	10.00 to 12.00	10.30 to 12.30
SECOND	12.30 to 14.30	13.00 to 15.00	13.30 to 15.30
THIRD	15.00 to 17.00	15.30 to 17.30	16.00 to 18.00

In the event of play being stopped for any reason the time lost will be added on to make up the two hours. If, however, there is ten minutes or less to be added then that particular amount of time will be subtracted from the total time of the following session.

Any impending imbalance in the time for the last two sessions on the final days' play must be rectified as far in advance as possible so that each team has the same amount of time batting or fielding. To the best of my knowledge a certain amount of time 'juggling' takes place already around about lunch or tea-time.

During each period of play at least a specified number of overs must be bowled.

If the specified number of overs is not bowled a suitable penalty must be enforced; for example for every over not bowled double?, treble?, the average number of runs scored per over must be added on to the batting side's score.

In its final session of fielding each team must bowl the specified number of overs or forfeit the match,

A Captain may declare at any time but having declared his team will not bat again. When one team's first innings ends in a normal way they will, after the usual time allowance, start their second innings and bat for the remaining time of their two hour period. It should be noted however that they may declare under the condition specified above.

The perceived benefits of adopting the general theme of the proposed rules are as follows

The advantage hoped to be gained by the team deciding whether to bowl or bat will hopefully be minimal. For example if the pitch is noted for being lively during the first session of play each day then on the second day a different team will be fielding. Also if the pitch is known to favour the spinners as it wears then one team alone will not benefit from this.

In test matches particularly, though not exclusively, most spectators will welcome the chance to see all of the opening batsmen and bowlers in action during the day rather than one team or the other possibly taking a stranglehold on the match. The proposed format should result in a more entertaining contest.

In test matches I would like to see a little national colour allowed, in fact insisted upon. For example the shirt collars or the ribbing around the neck of pullovers of Australian players should be yellow as that seems to be their national colour. The reason for this is that with the increase in the number of test playing countries and of the series being played it should be much easier to see at a glance which team is batting or fielding. It is not easy keeping abreast of the players of every team.

As mentioned earlier I have had an idea re batting practice, I did try several times in a squash court with a tennis ball, space of course is a limiting factor. From the back end of the court hit the ball hard at the wall with the serving line across it. The ball naturally comes back off the wall whereupon you contrive to hit it back again. One can soon discover ways and direction of hitting the ball so that its return path is suitable for playing; it can be driven, cut or swept to leg. Pretty rudimentary it is true but it is under cover and better than nothing.

While indulging in such practice I thought that in a purpose designed space the wall against which the ball is hit should be curved on an arc of a circle of radius, say, 20 yards. If the batsman stands at the "centre point" the ball should more or less come back along its original path. The distance involved, 20 yards, more approximately approaches reality than in a squash court.

On a scientific or trial and error basis different parts of the wall could be inclined, both ways, to the vertical so that a ball hit hard high up the wall comes back from a more realistic height. In the squash court I used a tennis ball in deference to the walls and space but against a designed wall a more solid high hysteresis ball could be used; one thing I can say is that one's reaction time is enhanced.

I have also practised catching and fielding in a squash court, again with a tennis ball; throw it hard against the wall and catch or field the return; it can be thrown high up on the end wall so that the return path is more akin to a ball that has been "skied".

With a hard high hysteresis ball and one or two companions I can more or less guarantee very concentrated and very good catching and fielding practice. It should not take a rocket scientist's brain to devise a competitive game aimed at points being awarded for catching and fielding prowess.

Words of warning however, batsman's type protective helmets may be advisable as well as good protection for any lights in the court.

As a final proposal I suggest that in fifty over matches there should be four 'sessions' of twenty-five overs each, one team will bat in the first and third sessions the other in the second and fourth. This should help to level the playing field, particularly in day and night matches. It should also maintain the interest in some situations.

ADDENDUM TO CRICKET
ELIMINATE DRAWN MATCHES

The first test (2007) between the West Indies and England ended in a draw after time was lost due to bad weather.

As I write these words at 09.45 on Monday 28th May 2007 the second test enters its fourth day with no certainty that there will be any play. England was in a very strong position at the end of play on the second day but the third day was completely rained off.

This situation crystallised my thinking into a solid state from which to argue the case "put an end to drawn matches", however I add the rider "as fairly as possible".

All teams, International, County or Provincial can, with varying degrees of conviction, claim that in such and such a game they were the moral winners but, conversely, would have to admit that in other matches they were very lucky to escape with a draw.

The draw scenario has even more of a downside where a "let us play for a draw" tactic can be adopted as an aid to winning a test match series.

I am sure that the idea of teams occupying the crease for equal periods of time will lend itself to resolving the outcome of matches cut short by bad weather.

Just, in effect, thinking aloud, let the position be assessed at every stage where the teams have occupied the crease for the same length of time. This would be, ideally, after the first two sessions, the first four sessions, the first six sessions and, if needs be, so on.

What criteria should be used in each case? Number of runs scored?, number of runs scored divided by the number of wickets that have fallen? Or? Or?

To simplify this would be easy if the number of days for a County match was restricted to two and that of a Test match to four. This reduction is not essential but it would in some cases avoid juggling the times for the third or fifth days.

Yet another way would be to specify that County matches should, within the three days allowed, consist of six two hour periods. Test matches (five days) would consist of twelve two hours sessions. At any stage after the first two sessions have been completed the result of the match should be known but it could change after the next two sessions!

If nothing else the above points should form the basis of a good discussion. For example if a County match finished with a result in two days then a limited over match could be played on the third day.

SNOOKER

Very truly a game of great skill. I first played in India on a full size table in the sergeants' mess and did not display any potential. Many, many years later circa 1975 a full size table was installed as a recreational facility at a college where I worked and lived.

I and several other members of staff played on a regular basis once or twice a week, good fun but again I displayed nothing at all above average skill. As a hopefully humorous aside while on a short holiday in Victoria Falls I sent a telegram to a friend; it said "Come quickly, table empty. CHALK1E". The secretary who received it for onward transmission was extremely puzzled; those were the days Doug!

Doug was responsible for the best fluke shot I have ever seen. I was playing him and it finished as a black ball game. Doug had the ability to hit the cue ball extremely hard; he really hammered the black ball towards the left hand corner pocket in baulk, his normal "Calling at all pockets shot".

The black ball did not go down and then off it went "calling at all pockets". In the meantime of course the white ball was doing its own thing. I was perfectly positioned at the other end of the table to see the white ball heading straight for the centre of the right hand corner pocket in baulk and victory for me. The white ball was no more than six inches from the pocket when the black ball crossed into its path and was duly knocked cleanly into the pocket; unfortunately for me the white ball did not follow it in. As Doug racked his cue he came out with his usual "Not everyone saw it that way."

It would prove very entertaining I am sure to see or hear of fluke shots. In more recent times I spent about three years as a member of a country club on a tea estate in the south east corner of Zimbabwe. The table in the club was not full size but it was big enough to warrant a long "Four away" rest and its matching cue.

Every Wednesday afternoon was devoted to golf and tennis followed by a social evening including dinner. The snooker table was a big attraction for several of us. Two items of humour. Jack, who did not claim to be a star in our somewhat restricted firmament, had potted a red but having missed the following colour he moved his marker on the scoreboard and said "My score is coming along in leaps and ones."

On another occasion a helicopter pilot from New Zealand had watched as two of us finished the last game in a practically empty club. As we covered the table with the usual white sheet he said "Do you sleep here as well?" Full marks to him.

At this stage I had, thanks to my daughter and son-in-law, graduated to my own cue, a screw together type. A friend on an adjacent tea estate, who was into woodwork as a means of supplementing his income, gave me a very smart and ornately machined box made of mukwa. It would have been unique but he made himself an identical one! When we went to play in another country club we reckoned it was worth a black ball start as we walked in carrying our boxes; thanks Phil.

In, finally, getting to the point of this chapter let me state categorically that I have no intention of submitting any suggestions as to how the rules covering the basic game could be altered, it is called SNOOKER and at the highest level of the game very great skills are displayed in laying on or getting out of snookers and it truly is a great game.

I do feel however that as a game for live spectating and television viewers there may be one or two alternative ways available to keep the interest up and eliminate some of the time often devoted to the early battle to avoid letting one's opponent in. Just as an alternative method of play aimed at providing an increase in interest at times possibly for both viewers and players the following could be considered. At this point let this proposal be called "POT THE LOT".

The first major departure from the traditional method of play is that only one player occupies the table as he attempts to clear it; the balls are positioned in the normal way and the player's intention is to clear the table and obtain the highest score, ie 147; now it will quickly become clear to an astute player that to increase his chance of scoring 147 it may well be best to play the balls into favourable positions for him to achieve the maximum score just by making sure that each time he starts scoring he can achieve a red followed by the black; this from everyone's point of view is not desirable. In a game played the conventional way it can become a little boring watching a world class player taking red black red black with apparent ease; the major point of interest being will he achieve a maximum.

So how to make sure that the player whose task it is to clear the table tries to do so without obviously setting up the reds near to pockets. There are several ways to do this without infringing too much on the conventional way.

A. The match official must be convinced that the player made a genuine attempt to pot the object ball; if not convinced then the penalty is minus four from the players score. In coming to their conclusion the match officials should consider as to whether the player has gained an advantage by not hitting or potting the object ball.

B. The player's final score will be divided by the number of shots he played and the result is his score. His first shot when breaking is not counted.

FRED'S POT THE LOT

Another way of playing with only one player at a time is as follows:
    The table is set up in the usual way then:

C. When breaking the cue ball has to be placed in the (D) baulk semi circle in the usual way but it must be played so that it hits the cushion at the baulk end of the table first before hitting a red ball, it may also hit another cushion or cushions before hitting a red ball.

D. After his first shot every shot played must legally pot a ball; if it fails to do so four points must be deducted from a player's score.

E.   The black ball can only be potted into either of the baulk end corner pockets, the only exception to this being when the colours are being potted to finish the game.

F.   The pink ball can only be potted into the corner pockets at the black ball end of the table; the only exception to this being when the "colours" are being potted to finish the game.

G.   The remaining "colours" can only be potted in the middle pockets; the only exception to this being when the colours are being potted to finish the game.

H.   Each frame must be completed in twenty-five minutes. After twenty-five minutes the value of all balls left on the table, with the exception of the cue ball, is deducted from the player's score. The figure of twenty-five minutes needs to be reviewed ultimately in the light of experience. In either of the suggested methods of "Pot the Lot" the only time a "Snooker" situation can occur is when the player snookers himself; he will have to get out of it in the usual way. The match officials must be convinced that the player made a genuine attempt to hit the object ball. If they are so convinced then the player will lose four points if no contact is made with the object ball or if the cue ball hits another ball, he will also lose four points for not potting the object ball. If the match officials are not convinced that the player made a genuine attempt to hit the object ball then four marks will be lost and the cue ball is placed back into the snooker position as is usually done.

Several questions can be asked and answers given as to how to run a competition between various numbers of players.

Firstly how many tables are there available and how many spectators or television cameras can be accommodated?

If only one table is available it will be possible to have up to say eight players depending on how many rounds are played and/or in the time available. Strictly the players may only need to play once to provide a winner, ie the one with the highest average score if playing straight Pot the Lot or the highest score if playing "Fred's Rules Pot the Lot"

If two tables are available it would be fair if all of the eight players were to play on each table. In that case the players total score for both frames is divided by the total number of shots for both frames if playing Pot the Lot or a simple total of both games if playing Fred's Rules Pot the Lot

If four tables are available then each of eight players could play on each of the four tables and the winner is decided in the same way as above.

Just to give some idea of the time scale involved depending on the number of players and the number of tables let us fix the number of players at eight and assume that thirty minutes is needed for each frame. If the time allowed for the players to complete a frame is twenty-five minutes that will leave five minutes to effect the change over to the next frame and table.

For eight players and one table each player will play once every four hours.

For eight players and two tables each player will play twice every four hours.

For eight players and four tables each player will play four times every four hours.

Obviously the more times each player plays the more meaningful the final results will be.

An eight hour playing day with four tables available would enable another eight players to play or the same eight could play again.

There is plenty of scope for using a knock out system but I feel that this should only be used if there is a large number of players and that the number of players who play in a "FINAL" should at least equal the number of tables, that is to say that in the case of four tables any of four players could emerge as the winner. It would be an all action final with each player appearing on each table, in which case the final would take two hours.

In today's electronic age a scoreboard showing the changing scores of all the players, whether playing or not, should not be too difficult.

As pointed out earlier in this chapter any snookers will be accidental. I feel that the method I have called "Pot the Lot" does not deviate far enough from the normal game and will result in the usual red black red black scenario that the world's top players make look boringly easy. Anyone who has played the game knows that it is very far from easy and that the viewers are watching practically unbelievable skill as each shot is executed. As an example I used to attempt most pots very slowly, the main reason being to retain some control of the cue ball. If the pot was missed it usually left the object ball nicely set up for my opponent; if I tried to control the cue ball I missed the pot ho! ho! The top players do both at the same time shot after shot.

The method that 1 have suggested in "Fred's Rules Pot the Lot" should ensure a whole new ball game because red black red black fifteen times in a row will not be easy and in chasing a high score the player will have many decisions to make. I feel convinced that it will provide very good entertainment and that between frames there will be plenty of time for the so financially necessary "Commercial Breaks" without infringing on playing time.

The thought arises that matches between countries could be arranged with play taking place practically simultaneously at a venue in each country. Say something like this: Assume the contest is between Scotland and Wales and that the venues are in Glasgow and Cardiff.

Four tables at each venue: in Glasgow there could be two players from Scotland and two players from Wales and the same arrangement applies to Cardiff. To decide which country wins the scores from each venue are totalled.

All of the players would be in action all of the time and each player will make his own "luck". It could be interesting. There could also be other ways of keeping the interest up in such a country against country match, for example in each visit to the table one player from Scotland could be playing against a nominated player from Wales playing at the same venue, then the other Welsh player at the same venue and finally against the two Welsh players at the other venue. There would be plenty of scope for deciding results on an individual basis as well as between the countries concerned. Almost a man of the match situation.

ADDENDUM TO SNOOKER

Having "kicked off" as it were in suggesting different ways in which the game may be played I wish to stress very heavily that these suggestions are primarily meant to be a comparatively fun way of exploiting the fantastic ability that the world's top players possess. These ways are put forward with the firm conviction that they will enhance the standing of the top players in the eyes of spectators, television viewers and, perhaps more importantly, SPONSORS who are willing to encourage a few fun type competitions between selected top class players.

The 2007 World Snooker Championship provided sustained interest, great appreciation and enjoyment but several matches, including the Final, developed into marathons due to the excellent skill displayed in "defensive" play. This type of play was not only utilised during the opening phase but was used at any moment to "play safe", with the World Championship and a considerable sum of money at stake the players cannot be faulted for adopting such tactics.

Reverting to the theme of having "kicked off" I have thought of several other different ways that may be woven in to my previous suggestions to maintain interest at a high level and present new problems for the top players to solve.

Carrying on with the idea of one player per table let the coloured balls retain their usual value but change the location of their "home" spots. Black and Yellow exchange places. Pink and Green exchange and Blue and Brown likewise exchange places. If a colour is potted it is replaced in its new place. The colours may be potted in any pocket. Any shot, apart from the opening shot, that does not pot a ball results in a penalty of four points.

The following suggested method is for two players playing on the same table with the balls in their normal positions.

The basic change is that players only play two shots each time they visit the table.

The player who breaks must hit a red with his first shot, if he pots one or more reds without committing a foul he can attempt to pot any of the colours.

If he does not pot a red or commit a foul with his first shot then it is "assumed" that he has potted a red and he can attempt to pot a colour with a maximum value of five.

After these first two shots any colour may be taken as though it was a red and if potted it must be immediately replaced on it's spot. The player may then attempt to pot any colour except the colour he potted as a red.

The player who broke then has his second two shots, his opponent then has his second two shots and so on and so on.

As long as there is a red ball on the table any colour ball may be potted as a red as explained above. When the last red is potted with the first shot of a player's two shots he may attempt to pot a colour in the usual way with his second shot and if successful the colour is replaced in the normal way. From this point in the game there are two different ways to finish it, these are explained below.

The first way is, continue to let any colour be potted as a red, it scores one but is not replaced on the table, the player, if he has not played his second shot may nominate a colour and if potted it is not replaced on the table and it's value accrues to the player. If as the colours are cleared from the table one ball remains it will only be worth one point to whoever pots it This method of finishing should ensure a quick result.

The second way is that the colours must be taken in the usual order and score their usual value, snookers are possible and the finish may not be quick. Letting the colours be used as reds will curtail the defensive play at the baulk end of the table but there should be plenty of scope for clever play and the frames should not take a long time.

DARTS

Another game where the skill displayed by the top players is phenomenal and at times hardly believable.

At the very top level the players will often put three darts into the treble twenty several times during a match; something an average player may never do in a lifetime.

I would like to see it made just a little more difficult for the professionals and have two suggestions that would do this and one other suggestion that could be applied regardless of the skill of the players. Note these suggestions only apply to professional contests.

1. Move the "toe board" two feet further away from the board.

2. Move the outer circling wire of the treble "oblongs" three millimetres towards the centre of the board; call the result a "PROFESSIONAL BOARD". The third suggestion is aimed at equalising the number of darts thrown by each player during a match so as to eliminate the advantage of starting first.

3. If the player who started second hits the double needed to finish then he has won, he actually may have thrown less darts than the first player to throw but of course that makes no difference. However if the player who started the game finishes on the double he needed then his opponent will have one, two or three darts to throw depending on how many throws the first player had to finish with the normal double. If it is impossible to win with the number of darts allowed then the player who started first wins. It should however be possible for the player who started second to win; this is explained below.

Assuming the first player obtained the double he wanted with the first dart of his three then it must be possible for the second player to finish with one dart. If it is not possible then he has lost. If however he needed a double and he gets it with one dart the game is drawn. If the first player used two darts of his three to finish then the second player can win if he finishes with his first dart and draw if he finishes with his second dart.

Likewise if the first player used three darts to finish the second player can win if he finishes with his first or second dart and draw if he finishes with his third dart. Surely this method of deciding the winner of the game has to be the fairer way, and, I may forecast, it will prolong the excitement at the top level of the game.

Now much the same as I have suggested for snooker I would like to put forward a couple of ideas that should provide a challenge for the players and an entertaining variation for spectators and television viewers. Again the basic difference is that two players will not be contesting a result by playing alternately on the same board. One player will have the sole use of a board but, at the same time he is playing against one or more players using other boards, normal boards will be used, that is to say, not a "Professional" board with trebles of reduced size.

As with the number of tables available in a snooker competition imposing a limit on the number of players playing at one time so in a darts competition the number of players competing directly against each other at the same time will depend on the number of boards available. I will assume that eight boards are available.

Variation One

This will be a normal type of game but eight players are competing at the same time. There is no question of a very fast speed of play coming into any of the variations suggested apart from stating that there will be an adequate amount of time to throw the specified number of darts. In the case of variation one this is the normal three darts. All players will be throwing the "same" three darts at more or less the same time. Say two minutes are allowed to throw three darts. A green light will be shown when play may start and a red light will show when the playing time, ie two minutes has elapsed.

The red light will go out and the green light will show after, say, one minute and it will then go out after two minutes as before.

The game will continue as above and as the players finish with whatever double was needed the number of darts that they used is recorded.

It is suggested that the match consists of eight games, this will enable each player to play on each board. The match could also consist of sixteen games ie each player plays twice on each board,

With sixteen players and eight boards two heats could be played with the four top players from each heat going into a final.

It is conceivable that thirty-two players could compete in such a knockout competition on eight boards staged in one day. The eight players playing in the final round of such a competition would have each played in twenty-four games at the end of the competition, or thirty-two if the final is over sixteen games. The winner can be calculated in several ways:

ONE

The first player to finish scores eight points; the second seven points and so on down to one point, in the event of players using the same number of darts then the combined number of points is divided by the number of players using that number of darts. The winner is the player with the highest number of points.

TWO

The number of darts used by a player to complete each game in the match is totalled and the winner is the player with the lowest total.

THREE

The winner is decided on a "Devil Take the Hindmost" basis. At the end of each game the player who is last, judged by their total score to that point, drops out. If two or more players have equal lowest scores they must have a sudden death play off to stay in the match.

VARIATION TWO

This is a complete departure from the usual way of playing although I would think at times players may have conjured up something similar as a break from the usual method.

I envisage that if this variation is played by the top players it will become very competitive, in effect it is a race around the board.

In numerical order (and in single, double and treble order) the player must put one dart into the "one" sector, one in the double one and one in the treble one, then the same must be done in the "two" sector of the board and so on finishing with 25 and 50.

Any dart into a single, double or treble out of sequence does not count. A perfect round will consist of sixty-two throws. Here it is suggested that the players could throw more than three darts, how many more?, say six or nine. This will save time and should open up a few gaps in the scoring; it may make it more difficult to put a dart into a treble if several other darts are blocking it.

The same choices of how to score to decide a winner are open. There are arguments in favour of each. Totalling the number of darts used and letting the lowest number decide the winner would probably be the fairest but it would be difficult for a player who made a hash of one number to fight his way back into contention.

Possibly the same can be said about awarding points after each game according to the finishing order and the winner is the player with the most points at the end of the match. If a player scores just one point for finishing eighth in one game he can notch up an eight for winning one or more of the other games, at least it will give him a chance to offset the damage.

As with Variation One above eight boards in use at the same time will provide a good test for the players and a good spectacle for spectators and viewers.

Also there will be plenty of scope for electronic wizardry in presenting the game by game scores and/or state of play.

In addition there should be natural cut-off points for commercial breaks.

BASKET BALL

This will fall into my "I Wish" category.

Firstly I have never played the game and secondly I have never actually seen a "live" game, but the game very obviously has a great deal going for it both for the players and for the spectators or viewers.

From the outside looking in, as it were, I have two areas of concern. The first is that for the top teams it seems to be too easy to score points. A team rushes up to one end and scores, getting the ball back into play seems to favour the team doing so and they rush up and score and so it goes on. With scores up into the eighties and nineties there is often only two or three points difference and it can appear that the team that happens to be in the lead when the game ends wins. I know that is how games are won but the margin, as a percentage of the total points scored, can be very small. Why not state that to win a team must have a lead of, say, ten points. If that suggestion is vetoed with the argument that it may take hours to get ten points ahead then that supports the argument that the teams are too evenly matched, in which case call the result a draw, ho! ho!

My second area of concern is that undoubtedly the game really favours tall or, even more so, very tall players.

There are several ways to reduce the advantage of height. Two that spring to mind are to set the basket much higher and make a suitably sized semi-circle on the floor under the basket from which points cannot be scored. As played at the moment some points seem to be scored by a player dropping or throwing the ball down through the hoop.

Another way, maybe something like it is in force, is to make two or even three limits on the maximum height of players.

Just to illustrate this method I will take three heights:

CAT 1   MAX HEIGHT 1·75 METRES ie APPROX 5' 9"

CAT 2   MAX HEIGHT 1·9 METRES ie APPROX 6' 3"

CAT 3   NO RESTRICTION ON HEIGHT,

This will allow a CAT 1 player to play in CAT 2 and any player can play in CAT 3.

In all cases consideration should be given to the height of the basket and the provision of a zone beneath the basket from which points cannot be scored as well as imposing a drawn result unless a team leads by X? points.

A major driving force behind my interest is the need to get more people involved in sports that will give them an interest and much needed exercise and basket ball should be able to provide that insofar as there is plenty of sustained action in it.

Provision of large enough halls to play the game should not be too expensive and the hall can be used for many other functions. In countries where poor weather and long nights prevail at least the sport is under cover as are the spectators and officials.

SCRABBLE

This word game has stood the test of time. No doubt like numerous other people my wife and I became mildly addicted to it when it first came out, even to the extent of playing when I came home to lunch.

My wife is a secretary and also very keen on solving cryptic cross-words. My initial work experience was training to be a mechanic; this was followed by three-and-a-half years in the army, Royal Engineers and subsequently, while in the REs, as a round peg in a very round hole, my technical expertise was put to good use. This occupation and a binding interest in it did not particularly enlarge my skill with words and the spelling thereof.

Shall we say that for every ten games we played my wife would most likely win six or seven of them but there was no guarantee that she would win the next game, why? – because luck comes into it, the luck being whether one finished up with a greatly unbalanced selection of letters; this could happen at any stage of the game.

As a matter of interest, and it became something to aim for, we divided our score by the number of "turns" we had. My wife raised the bar to 36 point something or other, ie she had averaged over 36 per turn. Again as a matter of interest my mother wrote to us to let us know she had played SQUAWKED across a double treble in the lower left hand corner of the board, I think the K was the letter already in place. Of course if the competition is fierce one can be tempted to play a spoiling game.

My proposal to try and mitigate against luck is as follows:

Before the game starts place all of the vowels, blanks, Ys and Ss in one bag and the remaining consonants in another.

Normal rules apply except that for the first selection of letters four are drawn from the bag containing vowels etc., and three are drawn from the bag of consonants. For subsequent selections the following rules should be adhered to. If one has played an even number of letters, then equal numbers of letters are taken from each bag. If an odd number of letters are played then an equal number of letters are taken from each bag plus one extra from the vowel bag. Perhaps a table will help; it does not matter how many vowels or consonants are actually played, the figure of note is the total tiles played.

	VOWEL BAG	CONSONANT BAG
INITIAL DRAW	4	3
IF ONE LETTER PLAYED	1	0
IF TWO LETTERS PLAYED	1	1
IF THREE LETTERS PLAYED	2	1
IF FOUR LETTERS PLAYED	2	2
IF FIVE LETTERS PLAYED	3	2
IF SIX LETTERS PLAYED	3	3
IF SEVEN LETTERS PLAYED	4	3

If any bag becomes empty then letters must be taken from the other bag. This method does give a player a slight control of his fate.

A variation, of course, would be to sort the letters out, all the vowels only in one bag and leave it to the player to decide from which bag to take letters; no question however of looking at them as they are drawn out. This may result in a heavy drain on the consonant bag as the players try to get the high scoring letters or Ss – interesting experiment though. Perhaps one could try as per the original suggestion but if a player uses an odd number of tiles they have the option of taking the "odd" tile to make up the number played from either bag, this will give them a little more control of their "luck".

If four players, try the effect of using two boards and two complete sets of letters. A coloured dot on the backs of one set will enable the sets to be sorted out at the end of a game. The letters should still be bagged with the vowels etc., in one bag.

I have suggested that two boards could be used if four people are playing because it gets to be a little pointless in planning where to play only to see the openings used before it is your turn to play. At least one can plan an alternate place to play.

If a player uses all of his tiles then the other player or players should be able to have one more go if needed to bring their number of 'goes' to the same total as the player who finished first. Against this of course is the fact that the first player does not have the chance of scoring more by joining on to either end of a word that is already there. In championship events I assume that playing a "spoiling" game is all part of the tactics, interesting? For example if the first player only plays a two letter word it must limit the second player's scoring chances.

POLITICS

In all probability when and if a reader gets to the end of this chapter he or she can justifiably ask "How naive can Fred be?"

I do not deny the validity of such a question but nevertheless I venture into the very clouded and murky water of politics with several firm convictions.

The top of these is the premise that one of the highest possible honours that a person may aspire to is to be fairly and democratically elected, on personal merit, to serve as a member of a country's governing body. In the case of a British citizen this is to become a member of parliament.

Another firm conviction is that something better than party politics must be found, or to couch that in stronger words, it is essential that party politics be consigned to the dustbin of history. No doubt they developed to the prominence they now occupy due to very compelling reasons but surely they have served their purpose and their very existence could now be construed as contrary to democratic government and principles.

Many years ago the argument was put forward that in reality victory to a particular party was in the hands of, comparatively, a minority of voters; the so-called swinging or floating vote.

This was based on the supposition that many millions of voters would support one party come what may, and that many millions more would support another party, also come what may.

The million-or-so swinging voters were those who, depending on their circumstances, and/or judgement of manifestos of the parties, would not vote for a particular party "come what may" and it was their vote that tipped the scales of victory or defeat one way or the other.

In my opinion a major factor in deciding a person's decision-making regarding voting is an assessment based on how their affluence is likely to be affected. Again, in my opinion, the general affluence in the UK now is extremely high. This has resulted in a coming-together of the major parties' platforms and this is probably narrowing the choice for the swinging voters.

Examples of this can be surely seen in the word "New" as applied to New Labour and in Mr Cameron's concern about the "Working Man".

Some time after Mr Blair became Prime Minister reference was made to his son attending a private school. This fact must really go against the grain with many labour supporters. I am not disputing that parents are absolutely entitled to seek what they consider to be the best schooling for their children but I feel there is something a little offside when a Prime Minister of a Labour Government sends his children to a private school; to my ears it just does not ring true. If anything it suggests to me that Mr Blair carefully chose politics as a career that could lead to personal satisfaction on several counts. No doubt the same suggestion could be made about many members of parliament and other democratic governments world-wide.

History may well judge that Mr Blair genuinely advanced the aims of the "New" Labour Party and that the majority of UK citizens have benefited from his tenure as PM but one of the areas that has received a great deal of adverse publicity is the accusation of cash for honours. To how many people has this been a total revelation? It has been to me, particularly when allied to the fact that it has apparently been going on for years and years. Again, in my opinion, this is a very sick state of affairs. This is open to more feelings of unease when viewed against talk of squeaky-clean MPs and absolutely no sleaze.

The coming together of the platforms of the major parties has been referred to by me as being driven by the general affluence. Neither party will come out with a manifesto that is extremely right wing or extremely left wing and their candidates will not venture too far from the party line for fear of censure by the heirarchy of the party, that is to say, their individual thoughts will not be expressed even though the party line will not be the best for their constituency.

The thought that made me really dig deep into my mind was "Why are leaders of democratic countries often lionised or hated as a person, as an individual?" My thinking was that the leader had been elected to that position and that any action by the leader should represent the will of the majority of the population; the action should not represent the will of the leader himself, in fact there should be situations where the leader embarks on a course of action because it is the will of the population even though he does not agree with that action.

The leader's function, as I see it, is to act on the majority will of government as this should represent the will of that segment of the population each member of government represents. It almost seems as though leaders of democratic countries often appear to be dictators. If they happen to be the leader of a party with a very large majority in government then this tendency towards dictatorial action may be more pronounced.

PROPOSAL ONE

In my ideal scenario all members of parliament should be elected as members on their individual merit, not because they have been nominated by a particular party, in fact political parties should be discouraged.

PROPOSAL TWO

The elected members of parliament should elect a Prime Minister and all of the other Ministers in turn. The elected Prime Minister may not personally like the elected Finance Minister, but he will have to work with him.

At any stage, a vote of no confidence may be called by members in respect of any MP or Minister, including the Prime Minister. If the vote is successful the Minister or MP concerned must resign from his membership of Parliament but he may contest the resulting by-election if he so wishes.

Any Minister may step down from their position before a vote of no confidence is voted on and will not be required to resign as an MP unless expected to, that is to say, they are no longer Ministers but are still subject to the regulations covering MPs.

Proposal Three

As far as I am aware the voters in a particular constituency cannot at present force their M P to resign hence the following proposal.

If 1,000 (5,000? 10,000?) voters in a constituency sign an official petition for their MP to resign, then he must do so. One of the petitioners must deposit £1,000.00 for every signature on the petition with the electoral authority. If the MP who resigned as a result of the petition does not contest or loses the resulting by-election then the total sum of money will be refunded to the person who paid it to the electoral authority. If, however, the MP who was forced to resign wins the resulting by-election then the money paid to the electoral authority will be forfeited to the state.

In theory each of the 1,000, 5,000 or 10,000 persons who have to sign the petition should submit £1,000 to the electoral authority. In practice it would be better for one man to receive the individual fees and pay the total amount required. The thought arises that one person or a combination of persons may provide the total amount required; this should make it easier to get the number of signatures needed to force a by-election; whether or not this is desirable is debatable. It would be more meaningful if each petitioner had to pay the £1,000 but not everyone who is dissatisfied with the MP's performance may have the amount of cash they have to risk.

Proposal Four

When the above proposals are in force serious consideration must be given to abolishing general elections for they will not be needed. I do not think that M Ps should only be allowed to serve for a fixed term. If they do not deserve to be sitting in parliament then a suitable petition or no confidence vote can force them to resign. The same can be said about any Minister. They should not be restricted to serving a fixed period as a Minister. If in the opinion of all MPs, the Prime Minister is doing a good job and representing their views, then he should be allowed to remain in office for years. I do not subscribe for fixed terms in office by the leader of a democratic government, he or she may be doing a fantastic job. Remember they can lose a vote of no confidence or their constituency voters can force them to resign.

PROPOSAL FIVE

MPs should not be allowed to vote increased salaries for themselves or for Ministers. It is a particular hate of mine that members of government can decide how much they should be paid. Many governments do just that. I am also totally against any money that is raised by taxes being used to support political parties.

It should be possible for a system to be devised whereby the voters decide on suitable salary scales for MPs and Ministers and from then on it could be linked to the COL or put to a referendum.

SUMMING UP

The situation has developed where many many people have very cynical views of politicians in general, some even in particular. This just has to be a very bad state of mind, regrettably though understandable.

Politicians should be squeaky clean and any "sleaze" or other action that detracts from this attribute should result in an immediate vote of no confidence being called for or the MP should resign immediately and put his character under the scrutiny of the voters by, if he or she wishes, contesting a by-election.

The supposed best man or woman for the job should be paramount in the voting process in each constituency and in the selection of the Prime Minister and other Ministers and deputies for the Prime Minister and the other Ministers.

With no party leaders dictating policy, every MP should be free to contribute to debates and to vote as guided by his conception, real or directed, of what is best for the constituency that voted the MP into parliament. The word "directed" used above is chosen on the assumption that the MP has sought advice and/or sounded out the feeling in the constituency.

When the PM or individual Ministers are involved in international negotiations they have to be sure that they are acting according to the wishes of the majority of MPs. If needed they must delay committing the country to a particular course of action until they have again sought the opinion of all MPs as reflected in a vote or votes on the subject under international discussion. This is to say that Parliament is in favour of the course of action to be followed by the PM or Minister.

At any time an MP can face a vote of no confidence in Parliament or be forced to resign in compliance with a petition organised in their constituency.

It should be possible to do away with general elections and, possibly, the major disruption caused by a change in the party in power.

When any vote is taken in Parliament the members' names and what they voted for must be published as a matter of routine.

I have mentioned the role that I think affluence plays in affecting the way people vote, it also, of course, affects the way in which political parties or candidates pitch their manifesto or proposals to appeal to the voters.

Affluence is judged or assessed by comparing one's own perceived affluence with that of your fellow countrymen's affluence measured against the same yardstick or within the same parameters.

Then, a thinking person or group of people can make an attempt at comparing the general affluence of the population in their own country with that of the perceived general affluence of the population of other countries. This comparison need not be general, it could well be specific to an individual or to a particular profession.

Simple examples will serve to illustrate the points in both cases. A person in a "developing" country may rate their affluence favourably because they and their family have enough to wear and eat and that the head of the household owns a bicycle; they may not even think about the affluence in other countries.

People in the UK may rate their own affluence on a personal basis by the value of the house they own or are buying and the quality of the car they own or are buying. On a country basis, their country's affluence is clearly higher than that of very many developing countries but they may perceive it as being less than that of, say, America or Norway.

I have laboured this appraisal of perceived affluence as I think it has a great influence in the UK when applied to party politics. I feel that a situation of the "Haves" and the "Have Nots" could develop where the party that promises to protect the interests of the "Haves" will become firmly entrenched.

The "Have Nots" will comprise the lowly educated and lowly qualified as well as many immigrants from the developing and ex-communist countries and they may well find themselves in a hole that is difficult to climb out of.

This possible situation is a complete reversal of that which pertained for say at least the first 60 years of the 20th century when, I suggest, the perceived "Haves" were a decided minority. This, to me, is a matter of some surprise that any party other than a left wing party held power in the UK. One could draw a conclusion that a majority of voters felt that their perceived affluence was safer under a right wing party than it would be under any other. If that was so it would be interesting to know the thinking at that time; how was their personal affluence rated and why did they think it was more likely to improve under a right wing government than under a left? There can be no doubt that, materially, the datum level by which a person judges his affluence is now set considerably higher than it was, comparatively, a short time ago. A "Have Not" of today would have been a "Have" of, say, twenty five years ago. How many people are questioning the level to which the general affluence can rise in the developed world or in the UK in particular?

How many years ago did Mr McMillan state, in effect, "You have never had it so good." and how much "gooder" is it now?

What leaning will the government have that will pilot our path into the future along the lines that the majority of the population consider to be best? I would suggest that we need to view our politicians in a much more favourable light than we do now; that every one of them should strive their very utmost to represent the majority view of their constituents; that they all know that the other members of government as well as the voters in their own constituency can force them to resign their seat. The time has surely come for something better than party politics.

The following observations may be indicative of the "coming together" of the platforms of the major parties. They are observations based on various snippets of information that have surfaced on the nation's media in the last few months, say, around the end of 2006 and the start of 2007.

There would appear to be some serious inability to supply, on time, even the basic dental and medical wants of the population as a whole, often due to lack of beds in hospitals.

There seems to be serious concern that many senior citizens struggle to keep warm and even more concern that many are not getting the help needed to enable them to stay in their own accommodation.

There seems to be serious concern that the cost of travelling by train is becoming very expensive and that very often passengers have to stand on long journeys.

There is concern that some children are living in poverty.

There is concern that many children are living in overcrowded conditions.

There is concern that our servicemen, on grounds of cost, are not being supplied with the best equipment for the job in hand.

There are many many more concerns but the few that I have selected are, with the possible exception of the last one, typical problems that have formed the bedrock on which a labour party would base its manifesto. They are concerns that, in the main, MONEY SHOULD FIX.

Other snippets of information from the media concerned with money are:

Members of Government had voted for their salaries to be increased.

It would appear that many persons in the medical profession are receiving an income from government that is well over six figures per annum.

It would appear that much of the new housing being built by developers is of the one or two bed-roomed variety as there is more money to be made that way, a fair enough proposition if making a profit is the only consideration.

It would appear that one million pound annual bonuses are the order of the day with many top employees in the "city".

It would appear that many banks are making very satisfactory profits, billions and billions of pounds in total.

It would appear; if I recall correctly, that some of the railway and energy supplying companies have also netted very good profits.

An unbiased observer from outer space could be justified in asking

"Which party has been in charge in the UK for the last ten years, left or right wing?"

ADDENDA TO POLITICS

A recent news item (Mar. 2007) reported that the Chief Executive Officer of a Council received a salary that was £40,000 more than that of the Prime Minister. During the Pros and Cons discussion that followed one of the persons, presumably supporting the CEO's salary scale came out with the hackneyed phrase "If you pay peanuts you get monkeys". Of more interest to me would have been an explanation as to how that salary was arrived at. The report made me think that town and district councillors should also be elected on a no party basis and could be forced to resign by a similar, though scaled down, method such as I advocate for MPs. It also follows that any salaries or allowances that are paid to them and indeed to any Council staff should be approved or set by the voters in that area.

I feel, and in many cases it may well have happened, that serving on a town or district council is a conduit to becoming a candidate in a national election. Perhaps, in the course of time, serving as an elected member of such a local council could be a prerequisite to serving in a national government.

A news item on 29/03/2007 reported that MPs had voted to give themselves a new £10,000 annual "communications" allowance.

Contents of "A Few Wishes"

FOOTPATHS ALONG ALL PUBLIC ROADS

I wish that Government would pass a law requiring all of the responsible authorities to ensure that all of their roads, excluding special cases, shall have a surfaced footpath on at least one side, the footpath to be 1·2 metres or more wide and protected by a kerb 150mm high.

The authorities concerned must prepare detailed plans of how they intend to comply with this law by 31/12/2020. The plans are to be submitted by 31/12/2008 and must, broadly, show a yearly target they intend to meet to ensure that the work is completed by the specified date or earlier.

In very special cases the law may be waived as being extremely difficult to meet, for example a very steep road constructed along a cliff with a rock face on one side and a fall on the other. Another example would be large or historic buildings, but in those cases consideration should be given as to whether a one way system of roads could ensure compliance with the law.

Motorways would be excluded but dual carriageways would require a footpath going each way.

Numerous long term benefits would result from such a law.

DEAR SIR OR MADAM

The implication in starting a letter with Dear Sir or Madam implies that the writer is not aware of the gender of the intended recipient. I wish that there was a nationally, or even internationally, recognised and accepted polite way of starting a letter in such circumstances, a way that only involved one word after "Dear?"

SEARCHING LETTER FOR DATE

I wish that there was one place on a letter where the date on which it was written could be found. My suggestion is that it <u>must</u> be in the extreme top right-hand corner of the first page of the letter; it could appear more than once if the writer so desired.

While on that subject, it would be nice if the postmark on envelopes could also be always easily read.

LIES USED TO OBTAIN SALES

In recent days a national paper published an article showing the difference between advertised prices and final reality prices claimed by some airlines and holiday booking agencies.

Daily would-be customers are assailed by SALE PRICE, B O G O F, BUY TWO GET ONE FREE, ETC ETC. The sophisticated customer thinks "Who do they think they are kidding?" The answer to that must be that many people are being "kidded" into buying something that they did not set out to buy. The same argument can be used by prices finishing in 99p or even, for large purchases in £9, say £599 for a bed or £5,999 for a car. This particular "come on" has stood the test of years, maybe even hundreds of years, yet it is still used, so that suggests it is effective.

One large retailer, when pushing a price reduced article, does quote their catalogue in which the item was offered at the previous higher price; this, hopefully, is to be commended!

As a case in point, in recent weeks my wife has seen a large variation in the price charged by a very well-known supermarket for the product of a very well-known manufacturer. The last increase was just over 100% for exactly the same article packaged in exactly the same way! It is a coffee-based product, new to us, we like it but as regards value for money we are now in the dark and feeling a little miffed.

Surely some form of legislation needs to be passed and enforced to curtail these "come on" sales pitches because some people young and old are influenced by the thought that they are getting a bargain. In a somewhat similar vein are "phone in" competition scams and offers of prizes that "you" have won. One reads of people running up huge phone bills or actually being defrauded of their life savings

I have recently returned to live in the UK and so many of these scams or attempted scams are new to me, but nevertheless I think I can ask with some sort of justification "What sort of world are we living in?" This all leads to my wish which is that laws could be introduced that provide heavy penalties for frauds and scams as outlined above. CAVEAT EMPTOR, however, prevails.

FRAUDULENT OR RECKLESS BUSINESS BEHAVIOUR BY COMPANY DIRECTORS

I wish that public confidence in the ethics and management of companies could be justified and that legislation could be formulated and enforced to ensure such confidence.

In recent years there have been several very high profile instances where huge international companies have been in the spotlight as they have suffered massive losses or even totally collapsed in circumstances best described as highly suspicious. Very often the people involved, who should have been publishing warnings well in advance of trouble looming, emerge unscathed from the financial crash of companies and many laugh all the way to the bank.

Pension scheme funds have been used in such a way that even employees of longstanding have been left with a very much reduced pension. The shares held by investors are rendered valueless and countless employees lose their jobs.

Recently in the UK we have witnessed a savings club having to inform hundreds of "savers" that they would most likely only receive a very small percentage of the cash they hoped to use at Christmas.

How about a law that at the first suspicion of anything worrying or fraudulent, likely to affect the finances of any company or business in a major way, the Directors, Accountants, Managers and any one who may be responsible in any way are arrested and held in such circumstances that they cannot converse with each other or with anyone who has an interest in the case.

They will then be questioned about the circumstances leading to their arrest and, if thought desirable, the Directors could hold a supervised and recorded board meeting to discuss the crisis.

From that point the police will decide what further action, if any, is necessary.

Another aspect of very shady behaviour is shown by this paragraph published on Thursday, January 25, 2007 by The Daily Telegraph. I quote:

"Record fines were imposed on leading engineering companies after the European Commission found that they were part of a cartel that "cheated" public companies and consumers for sixteen years" unquote.

The fines totalled £4,944 million. Ten companies were involved. The main products affected appear to be electrical switch gear. One of the companies, at least, plans to appeal.

Nothing was stated in respect of anyone having to face being charged or facing a prison sentence.

The public must be thankful for the efficiency of the personnel who exposed and conducted this case, but I cannot help feeling that if the people responsible for establishing that particular cartel knew that they could face a prison sentence, it may well have prevented it being formed.

The thought of even two of the major food retail companies entering into some form of pricing agreement with each other raises many worries.

FRAUDULENT OR RECKLESS INDUSTRIAL ACTION BY WORKERS OR TRADE UNIONS

I wish that public confidence in the ethics and behaviour of workers and trade unions could be elevated to one hundred percent.

Circa 1950, I obtained a job in the workshop of a major U K civil engineering company. During the interview I was told, by senior management, that if I wanted to work there I would have to join a union. I agreed to this. I still have my card and, possibly strangely, I am pleased that I have.

Management obviously thought that being a closed shop was beneficial to all concerned. It was suggested to me, possibly by a shop steward, that I should go to a union meeting. I went to one; the members addressed each other as brother; it obviously did not appeal to me and, from memory, I did not go to another meeting.

Employment conditions at the company were good; as a fitter I qualified for a "fitter's mate" which was a surprise. The company also gave a financial inducement for good timekeeping.

Here might be a good place to state that at the age of fourteen-and-a-half, I started employment in the workshop of a firm that is now a major international civil engineering company. At that time, however, one did not get paid if off sick, and the total leave for a holiday was one week a year, unpaid. So I can fairly claim to have had a drastic, though par for the course, introduction to earning a living and learning a trade.

Undoubtedly trade unions played a major role in upping the conditions of work and pay for their members, and they still have a vital influence on the general wellbeing of their members, but now in many instances, their actions have to be tempered more and more regarding the general wellbeing of the whole country's economy.

What is disturbing to me, and in many cases it has always been obvious, is the ability of certain segments of the workforce whose "industrial action" can exert a very disproportionate influence on the wellbeing of many people. Often the workers concerned do not possess any great skills or qualifications.

On a broader scale, looking back, can one say that the British motor cycle industry was killed stone-dead by employees pricing themselves out of the international market and that the automotive industry almost suffered the same fate.

I would suggest that an attempt must be made to classify all jobs on a skill-rating scale; that those ratings are those acceptable to the industry or profession concerned. Having established these ratings, employees must agree to abide by them and also agree not to take industrial action to obtain higher wages or altered conditions of employment; a pipe dream maybe but, in my opinion, and make no mistake about it, the UK's position as a major global player is in more jeopardy than we realise.

On a particularly worrying note, I looked aghast at a report in a paper that BA cabin crew took an average of twenty-one days per annum sick leave. I would like to see a government enquiry into that aspect because, quite candidly, the mind boggles at the whole scenario exposed by that report. If true it suggests that a major revision of the consciences of all the employees concerned is needed, or that many of them should be declared medically unfit to work. Another major worry is whether or not that average figure of days off per annum on account of sickness is a 'norm' for British Industry; now that would be scary.

EDUCATION

I wish that the majority of us felt that in the main, education for all ages was pretty much on the right track. I was truly amazed, almost beyond belief, to hear on a television programme a few days ago (Feb 2007) that seven million people in the UK could not read. I would have been amazed if the total had been one million – but seven million is truly shattering. Surely something could be done to rectify that situation. Do people who cannot read understand what they are missing? There well may be a sizeable number who will never learn due to medical reasons of some sort, but in other cases something could be done to stimulate a desire to read.

A useful starting aid would be to list the words that it is essential to know and recognise and to seek the advice of teachers who have had experience in teaching such people. Something that I have thought about in the last year or so may well have a bearing on the subject under discussion.

The thought occurred to me, out of the blue, that there must be little areas in the brain that deal with specific subjects. This thought came when I took note of the fact that I have problems with spelling. I am eighty-years-old and must have written millions of words in my life-time, but 1 still struggle to know how many c's and s's there are in 'occasion' and 'successful' to say nothing of trying to decide whether a word should end in 'or' or 'er' or even trying to find out where to start looking in a dictionary to ascertain the spelling 'sigh col o gee'! A saving grace is that, generally I know when I do not know!

Another bearing on one's ability to spell is the influence of one's employment. I trained and worked as a mechanic and as such my contact with printed words was rather limited. Conversely my wife, who in the main has no trouble with spelling, trained and worked in secretarial positions and her contact was ongoing; printed words were part of her life.

At school I usually did well with arithmetic, particularly mental arithmetic. Note however the difference between arithmetic and mathematics. My composition was generally good but my handwriting was constantly in the two out of ten range – and it still is!

Recently a publisher (Country Books), sent me a copy of "Bright is the Ring of Words". This is a small book containing a collection of writing by Ron Ellis.

Mr Ellis is a very similar age to me, and he was destined to work in a local engineering company. He left school at the age of fourteen and, at that age, he bought six or seven books in a second-hand bookshop, mainly classics, and took them home to read.

Clearly reading, and presumably the desire to improve his life by doing so, was instrumental in his subsequent career, which was well and truly based on words as he became a journalist working for regional and local newspapers. He had broken away from engineering into employment that he was obviously cut out for.

I make the point that in buying those books at the age of fourteen he had shaped his destiny; how many of us from that era can say that?

Returning to the theme of little areas in one's brain that may be instrumental in one's performance in different subjects, it dawned on me that I, possibly, would always struggle with spelling; it also opened the thought that some people would always struggle with arithmetic and/or mathematics.

This thought process has been solidified by the letters and numbers show "Countdown". Here we have prime examples of ability with both spelling in the case of the letters, and arithmetic, not mathematics, with the numbers. The two ladies anchoring the show are both brilliant in their area but are often almost matched by the contestants. Recently there was an eleven-year-old boy who displayed an astonishing ability for both facets of the show.

Overriding all of the comments I have made about "Countdown" is the phenomenal aptitude some contestants display when solving the conundrum that ends each show. Nine jumbled up letters are shown and the contestants have to re-arrange them to form a word within a time limit of thirty seconds. Sometimes the contestants do not solve the conundrum and the audience is invited to try; normally someone has solved it.

However it happens quite often that the letters have only been on display for five or six (or even less) seconds and zap! one of the contestants answers correctly. These are the ones over which I have used the words "phenomenal aptitude"; my brain is still trying to register exactly what the letters are; their brain has seen, more or less instantaneously, that they can be arranged to form a word. There just has to be a little segment of their brain that is exactly tuned in to the letters and words waveband.

It would be very interesting to know if tests can be devised and utilised to see if a person has an aptitude or a blank for different subjects; these tests will have to embrace different age groups to be of use in deciding what special training, if any, is needed for individual students.

Other areas that throw up remarkably expert young people, are chess and music; grandmasters by the age of ten.

This particular "I Wish" started with the question "Is education on the right track in the UK?" There have been several shifts in thinking during my lifetime.

I just cannot help believing that at the earliest age possible the main concentration should be on the three "Rs", even to the exclusion of all other subjects, and until the individual students have mastered the basics of these three essential subjects to an acceptable level, they should not be allowed to progress to other subjects.

At this point I realised that I am guilty of a very basic error which writers are often prone to, the error being an assumption that all of your readers know what you are writing about. My error is an assumption that the expression "the three R's" is universally known; this patently is not correct so I hasten to explain "three R's".

Firstly I am not aware who originated this expression but whoever it was displayed a huge amount of tongue-in-cheek sardonic humour so:

The first R is for READING
The second R is for RITING = WRITING

The third R is for RITHMETIC = ARITHMETIC.

It is obvious that a child, teenager or adult with a good grasp of all "three R's" has the basic knowledge, the very foundation, on which to build their life in this modern world.

I repeat that in my opinion, until a student of any age has reached an acceptable level in all three R's, they should not be allowed or encouraged to study other subjects.

Again, in my opinion, great and studied consideration by all the people concerned should be given as to the ages at which subjects such as History, Geography, Biology, Zoology and Art should be taught as serious subjects to students.

Further consideration should be given as to whether a series of lessons on certain subjects could be formalised for all students on a "need to know" basis. When these "need to know" lessons have finished, the students wishing to specialise in certain subjects can do so and those who are not that way inclined, can drop them, but at least they have been exposed to the basics of each subject.

Take History as an example: What do fourteen-year-old students "need to know" about History?

I would suggest that they need to know, in general, those aspects of recent history that had a direct threat to the security of Britain and how those aspects developed and were countered. They do not need to know the names of British Kings and Queens and the dates of battles, long since buried by the passage of time.

So "I WISH" that there were standard "NEED TO KNOW" booklets on all normal subjects other than the three R's. Some of these booklets may well consist mainly of reference details.

Physics, Chemistry and Electronics have not been mentioned yet. In this modern age of technology they are vital subjects. Certain aspects need to be taught, even ingrained into students, as soon as they are able to benefit from such exposure.

I have advocated that the three R's should be a priority. If young students have to be given "Exposure Breaks" because their concentration level has been tested, then there should be a plentiful supply of "Toys" available for them to develop their creative and practical learning potential. Such "toys" as Leggo, Meccano, Scalextric and plain straightforward wooden blocks are ideal for this, as would be fairly large size "push together" plastic skeletons of the human body. I am sure my son gained a fair amount of electrical experience making his old Scalextric track, cars and controls function.

PHYSICAL EDUCATION

Recent experience and factors also suggest that all students should, unless there are medical reasons, be made to partake in activities involving physical exertion. These should be graded on an age-related basis and should be reasonably testing. In my opinion this forced and planned exposure to taxing physical exertion is required more and more as students progress through their teens. Many children and young adults take to such exertion as a duck does to water. With current talk of raising the school leaving age, I feel that for the future wellbeing of most students, and indeed of the country, the physical fitness of it's inhabitants is of great importance.

In regard to the physical fitness of students of all ages, I wish that government would introduce, without unwarranted delay, physical fitness standards to be aimed for prior to attaining certain ages.

The logical end could well be a certificate to show the results of such tests as may be decided on.

These certificates could be issued at STANDARD AND ADVANCED LEVEL, the standard levels to be aimed for at the age of between 15 and 16 and the advanced level at the age of seventeeen plus years.

I have suggested distances and times, but I stress that they are only suggestions: the times should be adjusted by competent authorities. I have used the Imperial system of measurement initially, but perhaps metric units would be better, particularly if such standards are used throughout the world; that could be another "I Wish".

EVENT	STANDARD	ADVANCED
100 YARDS	15 Seconds	11 Seconds
1 MILE	8 Minutes	5 mins 30 Seconds

10 MILES	90 Minutes	65 Minutes
20 MILES	NOT REQUIRED	140 Minutes
LONG JUMP	?	?
HIGH JUMP	?	?
100 METRE SWIM	?	?
1000 METRE SWIM	?	?
100 METRES RUN	17 Seconds	12 Seconds
1,500 METRES RUN	7 Mins 45 Seconds	5 Mins 20 Second
15,000 METRES RUN	84 Minutes	67 Minutes
30,000 METRES RUN	NOT REQUIRED	130 Minutes

No doubt there will be strong opposition to this "I Wish" on many counts, but I feel that the physical wellbeing of the nation would increase tremendously.

Government has taken up the responsibility for the mental development of children and surely they can take on at least some of the responsibility for their physical development and consequent well being.

Let me again stress that the figures I have inserted are just there as examples. Qualified sportsmen and medical specialists need to suggest the times for the STANDARD certificate that should be comfortably attainable by young persons of both sexes.

I feel that in qualifying attempts, there should be no question of the students racing against each other. In all but the sprint distances, this could be controlled in the following way:

Younger but experienced teachers or members of athletic/swimming clubs could set the pace as follows. One or two run at such a pace that they will achieve the standard with x minutes to spare. The students must not overtake these pacemakers. A further one or two controlling persons run at a pace that will just achieve the standard. Students will know that they must keep ahead of these STANDARD SETTING pacemakers.

A little family story that should slot in nicely at this point. My son at senior school used to hate the compulsory cross-country runs with a passion; they were the "DREADED CROSS-COUNTRY TRAINING RUNS".

Having left school and started work he slotted in with some other young people living in a house in town, our home being some way out of town. I drove into town for some reason in the early evening and saw a man running along the grass verge at the side of the road, my son no less, out training, ho! ho! Why? Because he was playing rugby for one of the league teams.

At this point I feel that I need to give a brief resumé of my education so that the readers can form their own opinion of "Where I am coming from". This is meant in the way that my background, my personal experience, may well have shaped my arguments a particular way and that present-day thinking is in no way parallel to mine.

I was born in Hammersmith in March 1926 into a working class family, the first child. My father died in 1929 and at the time my mother was expecting another baby, this proved to be a girl. That year was to be the start of the depression, and my mother must have had a very tough time in making ends meet. I have no recollection of my father, or indeed as it subsequently turned out, his side of the family. In later life I gathered the impression that my mother received little or no support from them.

My mother's parents were Roman Catholics from Ireland. For about three or four years in the early 1930's I boarded full time at an RC school in Littlehampton. The teachers were, to the best of my knowledge, all nuns. Again I have virtually no recollection of that apart from the supposed fact that the nuns kept discipline with the aid of substantially-sized pieces of wood, two inches by one inch in section, but this may well have been planted in my mind by later imparted knowledge – for remembering the sizes would hardly have been conjured up by my thought process at that age. I have no recollection whatsoever of being at the receiving end of any such discipline.

I can, probably, thank the nuns for a very well ingrained sense of right or wrong and fair play. This was also probably enhanced by subsequent exposure to Sunday school after I left the boarding school.

This happened circa 1935 when my mother married again and my sister and I joined her and my stepfather in a newish house in Hayes, Middlesex. My stepfather was Welsh and he was employed as a labourer for a company building houses nearby. Through the years he subsequently worked his way up in the company and, for example, he became their manager on an opencast mining site.

At that time there were many people from Wales taking up employment in Hayes. The town boasted several large companies among them HMV known as the GRAM, FAIREY AVIATION, KRAFT CHEESE and NESTLÉS.

The children of a Welsh family who lived opposite us were tasked with taking me to school. Wood End Green if I remember correctly, about two miles away; we walked both ways. One of the children was a boy a few months older than me; we became lifelong friends and were "Best Man" at each other's weddings.

The building estate we lived on was expanding and a new junior school was built on it; this was called Grange Park.

We moved to another new housing estate which was being built at Kidlington, a few miles from Oxford. While there I attended a newish school nearby – a country atmosphere.

Returning to Hayes we found that Grange Park had been tasked with providing the first two classes of senior education while a new Senior School was built near Hayes End. This school was Mellow Lane. I also had a few months at a school on Mersey Island, just east of Colchester.

The war started while I was attending Mellow Lane Senior school and for a time we used to go to the school in the morning, pick up homework and immediately return home to do the work given to us. This was because it was not felt prudent for large numbers of children to be gathered in one place because of the threat of air raids. In that regard, the area was luckily spared any widespread damage, although towards the end a "doodle-bug" blew up near the HMV factory.

From the junior school only one child from my class went on to a grammar school, the rest of us left at the age of fourteen.

I received my first exposure to what may be termed tertiary

education, map-reading for example., while training in the Royal Engineers and, later, a full six months course on engines and pumps at the SME in Chatham, Kent. This was followed by a three month course which basically covered the theory and practice of instruction. In my army service and later back in civilian life all of this training stood me in very good stead.

In Southern Rhodesia and Zimbabwe I lectured and instructed on practical engineering to students studying for diplomas in Agriculture. I was so engaged for some twenty-six years full time and three years part time so I can claim experience in those fields.

As we lived "in the sticks" for many years, my wife with the help of government supplied material and text books etc., taught our children for the first two years of their "schooling". This official government supplied a correspondence course and my wife's adherence to it ensured that when our children went to boarding school for the first time they had no problems slotting into more formal education.

My eldest daughter wished to become a teacher and duly attended a teachers' training college for the required three year course. She taught at several government schools for many years and then, married to a farmer, she ran a small school teaching young children, also with the aid of the government correspondence course, for their first two years prior to boarding school. She imposed a limit of ten children and was always at or near the limit. A friend, also a trained teacher ran a similar school a few miles away and they used to have combined trips and sports days. Government inspectors used to visit their "schools" and their pupils' tests and exams were marked by government teachers at the headquarters of the correspondence based courses. A fair indication of where there is a will there is a way.

Looking back on that era in Southern Rhodesia, possibly from a heavily biased viewpoint, I would suggest that the end product of the government schools there was, on average, second-to-none in the world. I have often asked myself why were the schools there so well placed to achieve the results they did. Possibly they started from a privileged position brought about by the "Colonial status" of the country and the availability of "cheap" labour to support the economics of staffing and maintaining schools. This question of "cheap" did not apply to the teaching component of the labour force. So what were the factors that influenced the good reputation that I think the government schools had earned?

For one thing most of the schools were comparatively newly built and, generally, there was no shortage of space for sports fields. Another factor that particularly applied to boarding schools was that the parents of pupils were often well educated farmers and civil service employees and their children had been exposed to their level of expertise and intelligence.

I feel that the pupils at government senior schools achieved excellent academic results as well as more than holding their own on international sports fields and in games, a possible exception being football.

Towards the end of my army service I began to realise that my basic education was just that, basic. The senior schools of my era had taught me where to put the decimal point and that 'of' meant multiply, more or less that was it arithmetic wise. I enjoyed school though and now realise that there should have been much more on offer, as indeed there is nowadays.

Shortly after leaving the army I did embark on a correspondence course of some kind, but as I had resumed my chosen sport of cycle racing training took preference over studying.

Having married and taken up employment in Southern Rhodesia cycling fell away and rather belatedly I started studying again, this time with a series of "TEACH YOURSELF ???" books; algebra, geometry, mechanics, trigonometry and calculus basically.

Over a period of time, with the help of correspondence courses, I sat GCE examinations set by London University in 'O' level chemistry, 'A' level Pure Maths, 'A' level Applied Maths and 'O' level Physics, all as separate subjects. I needed 'A' level physics but was not able to access a suitable laboratory for the practical work.

The teach yourself series of books I rate very highly; I enjoy mathematics but admit that I am not a 'natural' in the subject. This leads me to a matter about which I have very strong feelings. I feel that many people, after leaving school, decide that they need to improve their knowledge so that they can qualify for a better or more interesting occupation.

The various professional or trade bodies should spell out very very clearly the path or paths that must be followed to enable a more mature person to qualify for employment in the areas they are responsible for. In some instances these days if a person does not have a degree in a particular subject then he can forget about that particular profession. I know that 'times' have very truly changed but in my youth the only knowledge of universities that I had was the annual Oxford versus Cambridge boat race!

On a similar track today's parents are far, far more knowledgeable about the vital importance of education than they were in my era.

So, returning to the start of this particular "I wish", is government on the right track regarding education for all ages and if it is not then what is the right track? The correct answer to that could well be instrumental in determining the UK's position in the world and the prosperity of its population.

That reminds me of an anecdote. It concerned a very mature and respected business leader paying a visit to his old university. On studying the current examination papers on economics he said to the Principal who was showing him around "These are the same questions that I answered forty years ago." "They certainly are" agreed the Professor "but now the answers are much different."

This could be very applicable to todays economic world for there are massive unknowns to be thought through and planned for.

The Anglo American Company used to employ experts to try to formulate conditions and policy five years down the line. I heard one of these experts deliver such a report at an Agriculture Congress in Harare. It was extremely well received and 1 think it has become something of a text book on forward planning.

The thought arises that say five of the UK's most esteemed universities could be tasked with a project that involved forward planning for the UK's best course of action until the end of 2012 and extended to the end of 2017. Reasons should be given for the scenarios they forecast. They can co-opt anyone they like onto their team, their reports to be in by the end of March 2008. To clarify the above there should be five reports, one from each university.

Another thought that has whirred away in my mind for many years is "How does one rate a country's worth present or potential?

I have only skimmed the surface regarding the multitude of factors that need to be considered but in doing so I came up with what I think is a new word. This was conjured up as I pondered as to the value of a very large population. They may well be a drag on a country if they are not helping the prosperity of the country; will their thinking help the country or just their muscles? Another yardstick of course is their role in the country's security but here again thinking could be an asset, even vitally so.

The word I came up with is THIGHT and it defines a thought second, so what can the standard be, an individual's time to solve a simultaneous equation?, a quadratic equation?, an anagram or a cross-word clue?, or? Or? Or? How many thoughts per second to answer, ie solve those questions.

So how about government, a large company or a wealthy individual sponsoring a competition to answer the question "How can a country's present and future worth be assessed"?

Only a few more "THIGHTS" to go. What if, without warning, the British Isles were to instantly sink, without trace or tidal waves, beneath the sea? What would be the immediate and long term effect of this on the rest of the world?

If one likes, substitute any other country and contemplate the immediate and long-term effect on the British Isles in particular and then the rest of the world.

Last 20 thights, let us assume there are one billion people in China. Let us also assume that Mr Money Bags is worth 100 billion American dollars and that he gives 100 American dollars to each person in China. What will be the immediate and long term effects on the Chinese and world's economy? This, if nothing else, should put the question of personal wealth into perspective. Donors please step forward to sponsor a prize for each of the best answers to the above questions.

SECURITY AND RELIGION

Two completely different areas in the broadest sense but recent events seem to be inexorably meshing the two areas together, so much so that my "I wish" must be, or should be, foremost on the minds of millions of people and the wish is "I wish that I did not have the feeling that the world is teetering on the very brink of a war, maybe ostensibly, brought about by religion or, dare I add, the lack of it".

With the thought that such a war would most likely end with the use of nuclear weapons my next "I wish" is that every leader in the world should be compelled to read Neville Shute's book "On the Beach". I started to read that book during a Christmas holiday about forty years ago; I finished it, in tears, two days later on Boxing Day.

As an example I would think there is no doubt that Israel possesses nuclear weapons and if the situation was to arise where they, the Israelis, thought they were about to be wiped out then enough nuclear weapons would be used to make sure that they were not the only ones to be exterminated.

Down a different road but in the same vehicle I put forward the thought that while America may not be top of the pops with the populations of many European and other countries at the moment it should be borne in mind that in the immediate months, and then years, following world war two the threat of American arms, more especially the atom bomb, may well have preserved their safety for there was little else capable of stopping the Red Army at that time should they have decided to extend their zone of influence even wider.

Another wish is that I could pick up one small book and in it read an accurate and authorised explanation of the world's major religions because at the moment I do not know how many major religions there are and how numerically they are supported.

I do know that one man can speak for the Roman Catholics and one man for the Church of England. I do not know how many men can speak as leaders of the other major religions. This of course is a potential problem because I feel that all of the religious leaders concerned need to speak with one strong voice in prohibiting any act that kills the citizens of a country unless a formal declaration of war exists between the citizens of the countries involved.

Another thought that surfaces is how many persons making a good living from a religion really unreservedly believe in everything they preach; and while in this state of wonderment I wonder how many persons being preached to unreservedly believe what they have heard or are hearing about their religion. How many preachers or those being preached to are cynical about what they believe and to what degree are they cynical. Just a little or are they totally cynical. One will never know of course but it is a question that everyone should ask themselves.

One can often see, amongst those being preached to or who have been so addressed, absolute belief in their religion, their faith can surely be seen in their faces, such faith is rather enlightening, almost scary to those watching who are not total believers themselves. Also, alas, one can see the result of such total belief when watching news reports showing the total carnage caused by total believers who have given their lives in proving their total belief knowing and hoping that they have killed numerous persons. Some of their hopes may have been that they would not kill any persons with belief the same as theirs but with totally indiscriminate carnage chances have to be taken.

But such carnage that has already been caused will be as nothing when nuclear war heads are unleashed, for millions of believers or non-believers alike will not have the luxury of even thinking about believing or not believing for they will no longer exist in human form and they are likely to be the lucky ones. Read "On the Beach"; if my recall is correct Mr Shute did not state "who" started it but once started every one joined in. Perhaps everyone should be fully aware of the two words that I have used, those words being "TOTAL CARNAGE"

So "I wish" that, please religious leaders of the world, lead us away from the thought that the world is teetering on the brink of a religious war and please, please do it quickly and sincerely.

In ending this chapter on Security and Religion I close with "I wish" that every person in the world was able to speak their mind on any subject without any fear whatsoever. Freedom of speech is a cornerstone of democracy but the qualifying words "without any fear whatsoever" can restrict a person exercising this freedom to the full.

PRIDE

I wish to be proud of my nationality. I will increase the impact of that by stating "I wish to be VERY proud of my nationality." However I will immediately add a rider to, or qualify that wish by saying that while one's nationality is important it should not be taken as an excuse to deride other nationalities. I will also state that I am British first and English second, but it would be nice to say British first and British last.

We are divided up into four component parts as it were but it makes me very sad that this division has already lead to thoughts of real division into separate countries; can we think of a word to unify us more than has been the case in the past? Let us meet in sporting contests but be united in everything else.

Ireland is a very tricky question but try and imagine that one hundred years have flashed by and what will the people of our two islands think about the years 1900 to 2000 or more; how long will the question of Northern Ireland and Ireland be unresolved. It is ridiculously easy for me to write this but surely just on geographical grounds alone the population of Northern Ireland should elect to become part of a unified Ireland and what is more of a pipe dream is the wish that a unified Ireland become part of whatever name is given to a "new" grouping together of two closely associated islands.

But getting back to PRIDE and wishing to be proud of my nationality there are mountains to be climbed before we can be, I think, unreservedly proud of our nationality. Sure we can be proud that our team has won the World Cup at this or that or we can be proud of the fact that we have a new ace (no pun intended) on the world's tennis courts or a Formula One Champion Driver but we should be even more proud of a total belief that the game is the thing, not winning it but, as Kipling put it, "How you played the game".

Pride in sporting achievements is one thing but it is not the pride that I am thinking about for that is a pride that we should have nothing to feel "UNPROUD" about. In my opinion the list of things that we can feel "Unproud" about is very long even without thinking about areas where there is no concensus. For example "Going to war with Iraq without the approval of the United Nations".

The long list that I could start with, for example:

1   the need to build more prisons
2   the need to ensure that there are no areas in the country where citizens are afraid to walk for fear of being mugged
3   the need for ASBOs
4   the need for young women to prostitute themselves to obtain money to buy drugs
5   the need to wait a long time for an operation because one cannot pay for it

and so on and on. These, I feel, are some of the problems that have to be solved so that one can be PROUD of being British.

Not many of these "Unproud" areas will be improved without strong leadership completely backed up by the entire population. I will perhaps over-simplify that by taking crime. There is not likely to be almost total success in that very wide area until the population as a whole decides "That is it, we have had enough of crime."

Having made that decision an individual may go to his or her brother or sister, mother or father, son or daughter, uncle or aunt, friend or acquaintance and say words such as "I know you are involved with stealing cars, robbing old people, drug dealing, vandalising stations etc etc and unless you stop 1 will report you to the police."

If the person making such a declaration feels that they are likely to suffer physical injury by making such a clear-cut statement then they should go straight to the police or use a safe line of some sort to retain their anonymity. They will surely be justified in taking such direct action due to just feeling that they are likely to be attacked if speaking to the criminal directly.

This method of helping to stop crime will make some people throw up their hands in horror and make such statements as "That will breed a nation of "grasses" or even "Super grasses". The alternative surely will be to breed a nation of criminals. There are disturbing signs that this may have started; knife and/or gun-carrying gangs of ever younger people. Open confrontation of the police. None of these activities are likely to make the average citizen proud of their nationality. A topical case in point is using a mobile phone while driving a vehicle. If a law is passed then that is it "IT IS A LAW". This law is disregarded by a very large number of drivers, so much so that the penalties have been increased. This disregard of the LAW is very disturbing. Why pussy-foot with the punishment. If found guilty of breaking that law the driver concerned should lose his licence for three months for the first offence, six months for the second and one year for the third. The driver should not be fined, it should not be a question of raising money for the state. Losing the licence to drive just has to be a strong enough deterrent. Surely all laws should be respected unless there is an absolutely cast iron reason for breaking them and such reason can be put to the judgement of a suitable court.

If there is a more or less universal feeling that a particular law is unjust then it is up to the government to act on this feeling even if the only solution that government can see is through a referendum.

How would the majority of the population respond to a referendum on whether or not it is a crime to use a hand held phone while driving?

Until such time as every person in the country is a role model we will need role models to inspire different ages or segments of our population.

Here I would like to fit in a little private moan about a couple of pet hates as they may be small straws in a wind that is eroding our level of tolerance, even encouraging such behaviour, and that in turn leads to more erosion so, in no particular order:

1   At an award ceremony for entertainers a very beautiful woman wearing a very classy evening gown won an award. Now what man or woman can fail to be impressed with watching such a beautiful woman, so elegantly gowned, moving with grace on to a well lit stage to receive an award that shows she is far more than just a pretty face. Holding the award she states in a well

modulated voice "I am GOB SMACKED". Call me old fashioned but those words, for me, shattered the illusion into little pieces.

2   Is it legal to hear practically every swear word that has been invented beamed out on a national television programme, not once but many times? If it is then it should be made illegal and the punishment for breaking that law should be meaningful. As a child I did not swear but after starting work at the age of fourteen, as a trainee mechanic, I picked up the habit very quickly. Why?; because the words were used quite freely by most of the men in the workshop. However, as was the custom in those days (1940-1944) it was infra dig to swear in front of women or children, or generally, in public. That is to say it seemed to be reserved for working situations with only men present. If one has to swear those guide lines would still be valid.

3   Is it desirable for our elected leaders to be referred to on television news programmes as Tony Blair or David Cameron, why not Mr Blair or even initially as "The Prime Minister, Mr Blair"?

Is it desirable that members of government, industry, the health services or whatever be subjected to impolite behaviour by the person questioning them. These ways often approach harassment, belligerence or downright rudeness. This rudeness is often demonstrated by the VIP being forcibly interrupted as he is speaking. If there is a time problem then maybe the VIP should not have been invited to speak without thought being given to really narrowing the scope of the interview.

Several times I have been completely put off by the forcing attitude of the person interviewing the VIP as they interrupted him or her. This attitude is not conducive to the ingraining of a polite demeanour in listeners.

This raises another impression I have of the loudness of many of the shows on television. One cannot deny that *Strictly Come Dancing*, *Dancing on Ice* and a wide variety of quiz type shows are popular and deservedly so but the crescendo of applause (Is some of it canned?) and near shouting that takes place is surely overdone.

Another brief show that filled me with disgust over the attitude of one of the persons taking part surely was something that no one can feel proud of. This particular episode took place, from memory, at approx. 7.25 am on Thursday 8th February 2007 and it concerned a subject that deserved better treatment than it received. It was about the amount of housework that a man might do or should do in the house with a view to sharing the load.

I could not resist the urge to turn it off because of the very aggressive attitude of the blonde woman playing out one of the leading roles. That episode summed up my feelings towards impolite "Sweep all before it behaviour." I wonder if the woman concerned has seen a replay of it. I would like to know if anyone could feel proud of that show being beamed out to the nation. The subject under discussion was a worthy subject and it deserved being treated as such.

A fair number of such shows seem be driven by the maxim SCORE POINTS AT ALL COSTS and show the person being interviewed "I am not scared or overawed by you even if you happen to be the Prime Minister".

It would be instructive if a complete list of "I am not proud ofs" could be drawn up. If it was the points raised could be arranged in order of severity and government and the nation could start rectifying them and ticking them off one by one and consigning them to history. Not many of these "Unprouds" will fade away on their own.

AFRICA

Having lived and worked in Africa from 1952 to 2005 I naturally have so many "wishes" that it is difficult to know where to start. So how did it start? That is easy to answer. I saw an advertisement in the *News Chronicle*, placed by the Southern Rhodesian Government inviting persons to apply for positions as petrol or diesel mechanics in their Central Mechanical Equipment Department. I applied, was accepted and duly arrived there in April 1952.

Now, with the benefit of hindsight, I can say to myself "I wish that I had never gone there" and then explain to myself that wish was because the end result was that fifty odd years of my economic life has been virtually wiped out by the "winds of change" that swept through Africa.

To qualify the "I wish" in the previous paragraph I should add that leaving aside the economic effects I must state very firmly that my family and I have been enriched in many other ways by the experience of living through fifty plus years in Central Africa.

For much of the time I played my very small part in developing the infrastructure of a modern state and the same can be said about thousands of artisans and engineers from all of the disciplines; this, unknowingly, was an enriching experience.

In the similar vein of enriching experiences one can list the sheer space available, the sunshine and the tremendous variety of climatic conditions provided by meaningful changes in altitude. Huge tracts of land at about 1,400 feet balanced by vast expanses at about 4,500 feet and much of the Eastern Highlands of Zimbabwe even higher with peaks at 6,000 to 8,000+ feet. Associated with these drastic changes in altitude of course there are similar drastic changes in temperature and, in many locations, rainfall.

Now as I work towards another "I wish" I must grasp the nettle of race relations. This, as history now relates, was a fairly nasty nettle in Zimbabwe and, indeed, during that same 50+ years, in the rest of the world. (It still is!)

Two little stories. On my first day's employment in Southern Rhodesia I was working on a bulldozer and the tea buzzer went. I said to the unskilled African working with me "Come, let's go to tea" whereupon another white mechanic said to me "No, it does not work like that here." The Africans went to tea in a different place to the white mechanics.

Years later I felt the need to write to the white Prime Minister. The gist of the letter was to the effect of "How can an African, living in his own country, be denied the right to buy a house wherever he wished?" At that time even the Asians had their "own" area in which to build. This was on the western edge of Salisbury and there were numerous magnificent houses built there. In short Africans were not allowed to build in European areas.

Just to dispel any thoughts that 1 must have been a dyed in the wool Liberal I will state that I also spent twenty plus years in the Police Reserve. During that time I did not, knowingly, see a terrorist or a freedom fighter although many of them may have seen me.

In general terms I like to think that a genuine feeling of goodwill existed between the races for many many years but, as a great poet wrote "The Moving Finger Writes…"

After a few years working alongside Africans of that era I had the thought "They may not eat with knives and forks, they may not have a handkerchief in their pocket but they are gentlemen in the true sense of the word."

I have been writing these last few pages on a race relationship basis but one can also embrace a person's ethnic roots. In that respect, a few months ago I was very moved, emotionally moved, by the following incident.

The driver of a mail order company's delivery truck called; when I opened the door we spoke to each other and then he said something like "That is very nice music" and I was able to reply that it was Deanna Durbin.

He was a young looking man, say 25 or so. On account of his accent I asked him where he came from and he replied "Turkey".

I was feeling rather surprised that a young man from Turkey appreciated such a recording from a long since gone era and I asked him why he liked it and he replied something such as "It moves one inside." I wish that I had a more definite recall of what exactly was said but when he left I thought over the moment and realised that it had been totally unexpected and very surprising and feeling unexpectedly "choked" I tried to get my thoughts into some semblance of order and ended up by thinking that somehow I needed to reappraise my attitude, my perception, of other ethnic persons; rather enlightening.

This also leads me to an "I wish" and this particular wish is that everyone in the world should think "I must not judge a person by their ethnicity or the colour of their skin but I should take note of the colour of their heart".

Using two words that can be taken to mean the same thing just to illustrate the point I will state that voluminous tomes have been written and no doubt will be written, about the history of Africa. I will make no attempt to add to these volumes apart from stating a few things that I think to be very relevant.

1   Africa is a text book example of the strong dominating the weak by force of arms. This domination was not just White on Black, it was Brown on Black and Black on Black. This domination by force of arms, was, and probably still is, par for the course throughout the world.

2   Slavery was a particularly very, very nasty manifestation of the force of arms.

3   The Europeans carved up and colonised most of Africa.

4   The majority of the countries colonised would not get their freedom without fighting hard for it.

5   Four above particularly applied to Zimbabwe and the two liberation parties received massive support from two of the world's major powers. Here I will slip in a statement I believe attributed to Sir Roy Welensky and a "joke" by a person unknown.

The statement was "One man, one vote, once." And the "joke" went something like this. "The colonial powers raped, pillaged and developed the countries they colonised. Liberation governments then took over and raped and pillaged their countries."

Notwithstanding the above my wish is that Africa could learn the lessons of the rest of the world and set about ending the turmoil that engulfs much of the continent. What opportunities there are to better their lives; the space that is available, the resources that are available. The virtually unlimited scope there is for tourism and development.

A very famous black American "Had a Dream". My dream is for three or four first class roads running the length of the continent and, say, six such first class, roads running from East to West. These roads could be backed up by railways and I would think that the development made feasible by such aids to moving goods and people would be enormous.

I wish there was a young African leader with the stature of Mr Mandela who could lead the continent away from the never ending fighting that threatens to destroy it.

A person who had lived there for a long time once said to me that Africa was like a bottomless pit and that all of the aid that could be given to it would just disappear into that pit virtually without trace. Africa needs to give the lie to that suggestion and to fill the pit in themselves and replace it with a continent that they can be rightly proud of. Where is/are the leader or leaders who can achieve this transformation?

Addendum to Education

The thought arises that other sporting bodies may think that standards could be set to cover their particular areas of interest, rowing and cycling are two examples. These sports however require the use of specialised equipment and I feel that they should not be compulsory standards. However the idea of other physical activities that are aimed at developing staying power, muscles and the confidence that such attributes can foster is, surely, sound. Following the above through, the controlling bodies of other sports could be invited to submit their ideas as to how they could go about promoting their particular sport with the aim of setting standards that senior school students should aim for

I believe data is available on expected life spans of persons who have competed seriously in various sports, there is also probably information on the general health of persons who have partaken in sporting or other activities that involved sustained and steady physical exertion. Such information could well be very enlightning.

EPILOGUE
ADDENDUM TO ADDENDA

APROPOS FOOTBALL

The first 30 minutes, at least, in the new Wembley Stadium when Chelsea played Manchester United for the FA cup provided assault proof examples of the time wasting tactic of passing the ball backwards and forwards while in one's own half of the field, and even more annoyingly, passing it back into the same half from a position well inside the opposing sides half. How totally different that game would have been if that type of negative play was not allowed.

Here could well be an appropriate place to think about the huge sums of money paid to talented people in various popular sports and games. Did the players in the cup final mentioned above give good value for their money? One goal in two hours play, much of it negative. Sure it would have been nice to have won but I can cry all the way to the bank. Perhaps the television companies, advertisers and various sponsors who are pumping so much money into various sports ought to be more concerned about the overall needs of the people watching and play their part in suggesting beneficial changes.

APROPOS COMPANY BEHAVIOUR

From a newspaper on Sat. 19th May 2007.

BA expects to pay £350m for price fixing scandal. Directors could face jail sentences of five years and unlimited fines.

APROPOS POLITICS

Remarks regarding The Freedom of Information (Amendment) Bill. "Shameful day for democracy."

"Anger as MPs vote to keep their spending secret from you."

"Smug, self serving and out of touch."

"Rarely has the seediness of our political cadre been so nakedly demonstrated".

"The House of Commons yesterday witnessed the kind of shabby, devious behaviour that would make the dictator of a banana republic blush". My suggestion that voters should be able to force their MPs to resign may have prevented that bill from even being proposed!

APROPOS EDUCATION

Half a million people have dropped out of adult education classes after the costs soared by a third.

APROPOS FEELING "UNPROUD"

"Strongman who lifted a fortune in disability allowances" The paper quoted benefits of £43,000.

REPORTS IN RECENT NEWSPAPERS

In two separate cases people were found guilty of lying in court. One of them was an extremely rich woman. On appeal three judges reduced the short prison sentence that she had been given. One out of every eight days claimed off sick by British workers was a false claim.

A FINAL (FOR NOW) "I WISH"

I wish that the top brains in the world should, in conjunction with each other, be asked to devote all of their time to formulating advice as to how to tackle the different behavioural problems facing the world.

These problems should be listed and dealt with one by one.

At the top of the list could be "How to install a heightened sense of conscience, the sense of right and wrong in individuals? The hope will be that such a heightened sense will lead to universal conscientious behaviour.